CHRISTIANITY
AND
est

By Max B. Skousen

DeVorss & Company, Publishers
P.O. Box 550
Marina del Rey, California 90291

ISBN: 0-87516-250-9

Library of Congress Card Catalog Number: 77-91635

Printed in the United States of America
by Book Graphics, Inc., Marina del Rey, California

CONTENTS

CHAPTER 1
Introduction

"est" came into being in 1971. Its impact on the lives of those who experienced the est training gradually inspired and provoked increasing coverage in magazine articles, press reports and radio/television interviews. Then in 1976 came the books on est. Nine of them in one year. All that I have read were written knowledgeably by people who had taken the training and could write from first-hand experience. As a matter of fact, it was through one of these books that I went from curiosity about est to a determination to try it for myself. So I am very appreciative of the great contribution that has been made by these writers. They have written frankly, expressing both positive and negative reactions from their own experiences as well as from those graduates whom they interviewed.

I have heard that many graduates would like to become est trainers, just as many "could write a book." All of this surge of creativity is just another demonstration that the est training does tend to get people moving with their lives. In contrast to the other nine books, this book is not specifically about the est training. Instead it has much more to do with what happened with est and Werner Erhard in 1976 after the other books were written. Werner calls what happened "The Transformation of est." Many of the questions raised by the writers of the books and articles were answered in what took place that year.

The defined purpose of the est training is "to transform your ability to experience living." Most of

1

the authors report that they found this occurring to a remarkable degree in themselves and in others. They also dealt with the less positive reaction many graduates had to the structure and function of the est organization. These criticisms added to the concern many had about the true motives of the founder. I think it was appropriate and fortunate that these detailed observations were recorded showing the apparent inconsistencies between the est training and the est staff. These writers were experiencing the est organization when, in the words of Werner, "a crystallization of evil" was coming to a climax. He defines evil as trading aliveness for survival. Another way to put it is trading joy and satisfaction for the gratification of being right. Evil is manifest in an institution when it moves away from its valid purpose in order to survive. In other words, an organization ceases to exist as a way of serving individuals and survives by being served instead, requiring the control and sacrifice of people for success.

Early in 1976 Werner Erhard was brought to a confrontation with this growing "evil" in est. In doing so he took responsibility for a major redirection designed to reverse the trends that many people, including many of the staff, had found so objectionable. More than that, however, is that in doing what he did, Werner clarified openly what he is intending to be doing through est, what he is really committed to and from where he comes. It appears to me that Werner is involved in something much more than transforming our ability to experience living—great as that may be. In addition, even primarily, he is dealing with the transformation of the whole self—

individually and collectively. In this area we are talking about something which is totally spiritual. It has to do with much more than transforming some thousands of lives. His purpose is to assist in a meaningful way in the transforming of society, itself.

Of course such a worthy aim is not new. This was the promise of Christianity two thousand years ago when the angel heralded the glad tidings of peace on earth and good will to men. Yet during these last two thousand years, the record of Christianity as a purifying process has been mixed. Certainly all would agree that it has made a great contribution even while functioning below its potential. So the question can be asked, is est in competition with Christianity? Is it a spiritual substitute or false imitation?

My answer is that it is none of these. The true mission of Christ was to provide a miraculous TRANSFORMATION in the lives of those who received him. The difficulty that Christianity has experienced during the last two thousand years comes from the number of Christians who failed to experience the gift of the spiritual rebirth. So Christianity, meaning those people who have subscribed to a belief that they should follow Christ, has not been able to unite the world and, due to the many divisions in Christianity, has been in many ways bringing about division.

Transformation is to move from dis-unity to unity. It means to be transformed, literally reborn, from disintegration and fragmentation to oneness and union. This is a process which can take place individually and collectively, by one or by the whole. When Christ spoke of the power that could and would do this, he defined it as a certain kind of love. So does Werner. Regeneration means to go from fear to love. That is what est is all about, just as it is what Christianity is all about. Therefore, since love is never in competition with anything, even hate, est and Christianity really support each other.

The problems that est got into during its first four years happened to be some of the same problems that Christianity got into many centuries ago. Both got involved with the enforcement of authority to protect the institution, all done in the name of what is "good and right." Being good and right always co-exists with fear. *Agape* is the Greek word which describes the specific kind of love Christ was talking about. It does not co-exist with fear. As John the Beloved strongly proclaimed, "Perfect love (agape) casts out fear because fear is torment and he that feareth is not yet made perfect in love (agape)."[1]

In 1976, Werner found it appropriate to take the lead in the transformation of the organization of est. The short five year story of est can be paralleled with the two thousand year story of Christianity. There, too, rigidity and crystallizations have taken place. What Werner did to est, which he called "getting off it and getting on with it," Christians can and may do for the church. That is what this book is about. This is not a call to revival. It is a call to examining the barriers that stand in the way of experiencing the gift of eternal life which is already ours.

The title, *Christianity and est*, suggests that there is a meaningful relationship between the two. It is my point of view that each can make a significant contribution to our understanding and/or appreciation of the other. Therefore, to the est graduate, the book is intended to amplify the est experience through some often overlooked teachings of Jesus, and in doing so, increase the individual's appreciation of our rich Christian heritage. On the other hand, to a believing Christian who is curious about est, the book is designed to show the way est can serve the individual in more completely fulfilling the promises made by Christ to those who truly become one with him.

---

1. I John 4:7. King James Transl.

CHAPTER 2

est — An Experience

I want to make a statement about est from my point of view. For me, est is an organization which provides a valuable and miraculous product. The product is not religion, philosophy, psychology, therapy, or happiness, although I also realize that most people want one or more of these when they go to the est training. The product or purpose as Werner Erhard defines it is about transformation. Regeneration, which is another way to say it, cannot be learned nor taught. It does not change the conditions and circumstances in our lives so that they fulfill our preconceived idea of the ideal. What it does do is make us alive in a different way than we dreamed possible and that is a valuable miracle.

Down through the ages and in many parts of the world there have been some carefully guarded teachings which state that man is actually totally different from what he thinks himself to be. Even though man may often believe he will be a spirit in the next world, he identifies in this life as being his mind and his body. Thus he believes he is only as smart as his mind thinks and only as happy as his body feels. In contrast, the ancient teachings disclose the possibility that there is a higher state of being which goes beyond the limitations and confinement of the mind and body. This higher state is not mystical or aloof from reality. It is merely a totally different way of experiencing living. In this state, one is in touch with the essence of life, itself, which is experienced in complete union, without division. In this level of direct experience, all the manifestations of fear, such as hate, guilt, resentment and greed, cease to exist. What does exist is agape-love, without fear.

Most of us have become totally conditioned to live through the mind, trying to find the answers to fear. Yet the mind is not capable of functioning without fear except on a temporary basis, particularly when altered by a trance-hypnotic state or by drugs. The world has greatly resisted this ancient wisdom which persistently surfaces to proclaim that man is an un-limited function of infinite being. As such, man is actually total and complete right now. However, since he unconsciously identifies himself as being his mind and body, which are finite and inadequate, he thinks of himself as being the same way. He is constantly struggling to become something really worthwhile so that he can overcome the feeling that he is an inadequate THING. All this is the mind resisting awakening from the thing-illusion and to experience being a NO THING. The teachings state that BEING is not a thing. Being is this totally incomprehensible and incredible aspect of existence called LIFE.

So now we come back to est. The est product is to provide a process that will de-hypnotize our minds long enough so that we can experience directly just being. It is called "getting it." It is to experience being as NO THING. The first experience of this may be very brief, yet the impact of the experience cracks to some extent the solid wall of sleep. After the training, "getting it" will reoccur from time to time just in the process of living. This repeated ex-perience softens the wall or barrier until it may suddenly and totally disappear. It just takes place.

"Trying" to make one's barriers disappear is the surest way in the world to keep it from happening. So the est seminars are carefully designed to catch the mind off guard. This may be the reason Werner considers boredom to be a very favorable state of consciousness. The training provides abundant opportunity for that to take place.

The training consists of a great deal of lecture material referred to as "data." These "notions" of est are acknowledged as "metaphysical horseshit." Since the data is presented very forcefully and authoritatively, people are confused by the apparent contradiction. Most trainees find much of the data terrific. I certainly did. Then why is it bad? Werner does not say the data is bad. He said it is metaphysical, meaning beyond the physical, and horseshit, which means horse manure. Manure is not bad. As a matter of fact, it is very useful to enable other things—very different things—to grow. That is the way with the est data. He stresses that understanding the concepts is to win the booby prize. However, allowing the data to just be there can provide the nourishment necessary for a direct experience of the self—apart from the mind. Then a very different state of being is directly experienced.

There are usually 250 people in a training seminar and they will get 250 unique and different experiences of the training. All are frequently reminded to "follow instructions and take what you get." I am clear that no one experienced the training in exactly the same way I did. This is not to say that my particular experience was better. It was just different. During and after the training, there are many opportunities for sharing by those who wish to communicate their particular experiences. Sharing produces value in that it expands one's own experience to include, to some degree, what others have discovered. So for you who are graduates, this book is my opportunity to share some aspects of my own experience. To you who have not had the training, although this material can in no way substitute for the direct experience, it may increase your understanding that the training is consistent with your search for total spiritual fulfillment.

I went to est with a very satisfying background in Christian experience. Although I had maintained a successful business career for many years, my first love was always the study and teaching of the Gospel. I enjoyed teaching and lecturing around the country, along with producing a number of books on the process of spiritual attainment, or as some like to call it, growing in grace and sanctification.

Yet, with all the satisfaction I experienced in church service and gospel teaching, I was still aware that Jesus had promised a level of spirituality and Godliness which I had not fully found. For example, there was this emphasis on perfect love which casts out all fear. I understood how the mind tries to suppress fear or deny its existence through disguises, claiming it to be righteous concern. But anxiety and worry are just other names for fear. Even the need for spiritual attainment is rooted in fear.

Over the years, there were many personal breakthroughs which provided much spiritual growth. Then about ten years ago I began to get acquainted with teaching material which dealt with those barriers we all have to this higher state of consciousness. Some of the material was within the Christian tradition while some was from different religious backgrounds. I was amazed to find that the different sources were all teaching the same revolutionary message—that the true self in man is singular, perfectly complete and there are only barriers to his experiencing his perfection. The teachings did not deal with how to become perfect or get perfection, merely ways of discovering the illusions upon which the barriers to experiencing perfection exist. The barriers were obstructions to agape-love. They were not walls to be scaled but mirages to be discovered and dismissed.

I found that Jesus had taught these ideas very clearly and I was surprised that I had not seen them before. For example, in the Sermon On The Mount, after describing the necessity of experiencing agape, which is love without any qualifications, he said, "Be ye therefore perfect even as your Father in Heaven is perfect."[1] The word he used was *BE*. I had unconsciously translated it to BECOME—out there some place in the future. I had translated *perfect* into being absolutely *ideal*. I began to discover that nothing is totally ideal because ideals contradict other ideals. Perfect does not really mean ideal at all. It means whole, entire and complete. In English grammar, we have what we call the *perfect tense* which expresses an act which is totally complete, such as "I have spoken." The *imperfect tense* would be "I was speaking" which does not establish completeness. The word in Spanish for perfect is *perfecto* and deals with all the parts being in place. Yet in English usage, most of us would think a person a little insane to declare, "I am perfect." We translate that to mean, "I am perfectly *good*."

The same principle applies to love. Love without restriction is TOTAL. That is why the mind cannot have agape. The mind deals only with parts, such as "us and them" and "becoming perfect" or "getting complete." It does not get wholes, such as "is perfect" or now "being complete."

So the way I experienced est is that it was not about becoming anything. It was about being and discovering that the barriers are only illusions we have created which keep us stuck in our preconceived opinions, judgements, fears and needs. Neither is est about finding the truth. It is about experiencing the truth of being and being is always complete.

Werner says that it is his point of view that we already have the truth. Here are his words:

> "In est, we're not attempting to give people material or information they don't already have. What we're attempting to do is to get them in touch with ways of knowing what they're unfamiliar with, what they've always had there but haven't perhaps been in tune with . . . We don't think we know something which, if you knew, you'd be better off with. We think *you* know something which, if you knew, you'd be better off."[2]

As Jesus put it, "Ye shall know the truth and the truth shall make you free." May I paraphrase it as, ye shall know the truth of what you are and the truth shall make you free in love without fear.

---

1. I John 4:17
2. New Age Journal

CHAPTER 3

Christianity—A Four-Level Experience

In contrast to est, Christianity is to most people a religion, a philosophy of life and a church. As such it is a set of doctrines, beliefs and commandments coming from a trusted source, the scriptures. Its central teaching is that mankind was lost through sin and required a redeemer, who was God Himself through His Son Jesus Christ, and those who would receive him would be saved to rejoice with Christ in the eternal Kingdom of God.

It is generally accepted that to merely acknowledge a belief in the New Testament is not sufficient since the benefits of the atoning sacrifice of Christ must come through some form of personal relationship with him and his teachings. From there on, the path becomes divided into many formal and informal differences. Even where all seem to agree that Christianity must come into one's life on the level of direct experience, there is wide variation as to what is considered to be the required direct experience.

It is not my purpose to take one position as opposed to another but to emphasize the personal value felt in each of the many ways Christians experience their religion. One can look at any of the denominations—Baptists, Catholics, Lutherans, Jehovah's Witnesses, Methodists, Latter-day Saints, Seventh-day Adventists, Pentacostals, Congregationalists and so forth. The members of each who are involved usually hold to the belief that their experience of the Gospel is at least as good, if not better, than any other.

I was raised and was very active for many years in one of the more literal denominations. I grew up knowing that not only was my church the best, it was also the only one that would do the whole job. It was very gratifying for me to realize that, of all the religions, I had the only right one. This "testimony" was based on the heart-burning conviction that my church had the only correct understanding of the scriptures, total reasonableness, real workability and satisfaction, along with true spiritual experiences. Then as I had opportunity to get better acquainted with folks in other faiths, study their teachings and listen to them enthusiastically describe their spiritual experiences, I realized that such blessings come in every denomination and every religion.

This is not to say that I still did not prefer one more than another. I just began to realize that finding value, confidence and comfort is not unique to the faithful of any particular group. Most people are convinced that their religion works in this life and will prove to work in the next. Some religions have more emotional things going for them, some experience more miracles and gifts, some require greater participation and sacrifice, yet almost all feel that their way is as good as any other, if not the one and only.

I wanted to make this point clear before dealing with the four levels of Christian experience so that there would be no question about the fact that I really support every person who is working at his religion. Of course, about half of those who claim church membership do not work at it and are really not that interested—at least not until some great sorrow comes into their lives. Of the other half, most care enough to get involved. In fact, between forty and forty-five percent of all Americans attend church at least once during a week. In a current survey, thirty-eight percent felt that they had been born again. A recent new translation of the Bible sold over two million copies within the first few months.

So there is no question about the fact that Christian churches are still with us and are a viable part of western civilization. However, certainly something is missing. Whether we look at politics, business, unions, entertainment, health, marriage, family, crime, education or any other aspect of our modern society, we see manifestations of division, contention, greed, cheating, inefficiency, frustration, fear and unhappiness.

Some time ago when I was leading groups in a spiritual insight program called Prayer Therapy, I formed one group made up of some of the finest people I knew. They were devoted Christians, in every sense of the word. As far as I had been aware, their lives were also prosperous, healthy, fulfilling and confident. In fact, as I planned for the first meeting, I felt apprehension about the absence of anything major to be accomplished. The groups that I had led previously were made up of troubled people who shared and supported each other in their mutual agony. This new group was already so enlightened and spiritually fulfilled, I thought, there would be little frustration to stimulate group interplay. Was I in for a surprise! I became amazed as the weeks went by to find that my friends in this group were just as frustrated as the others. The only difference was that they had found better ways of outwardly coping with their troubles. Many of their problems had been hidden from me as well as from themselves. It turned out to be the most productive group I experienced.

So if we were to ask the question, "Is Christianity working today?" our answer would be both yes and no. On the basis of whether we are experiencing the instruction of Jesus to "be ye therefore perfect even as your Father in heaven is perfect" and "peace on earth, good will to men," we must admit that it is far from working. Yet when we compare what Christianity has added to many of our lives, we would have to say, yes, of course it is working. The reason for both the yes and no is that the teachings of Christ actually exist on more than one level. We may be applying the teachings on one level, at least to some degree, and failing completely to apply them on another level.

Actually, it appears that the teachings are designed so that a person can find nourishment on whatever level one is at the time. Jesus taught large multitudes on one level and then would teach his intimate students, up to as many as one hundred and twenty, on a higher level. For the crowds, he often used parables about the Kingdom of God. Privately, he would ask his inner group what they got out of the stories. He would then astound them with a much deeper meaning than they had perceived.

The disciples were instructed in this way for three years and grew tremendously. Christ was able to give the twelve, then later seventy more, the power to go out to teach and perform miracles. When they came back from these missions, they rejoiced, describing enthusiastically how they had healed the sick, cast out devils, cleansed the lepers and confounded the "wise" men of their day.

Yet after all this, Jesus would still tell even members of the twelve that they were not yet truly converted, meaning really turned around. They would require an even higher level of teaching. At the Last Supper, the night before his crucifixion, he said, "I have yet many things to say to you, BUT YE CANNOT BEAR THEM NOW . . . These things have I spoken unto you in proverbs, but the time cometh when I shall show you plainly of the Father."[1] Thus he acknowledged that even those previous inner teachings, which permitted them to function with miraculous power, were at a much lower level than they were yet to receive from him.

During the terrifying events of the public disgrace and execution of Christ, the disciples experienced personally the shocking reality of their spiritual immaturity. As they later met with the resurrected Christ, it appears that they were ready to start listening without their false pride and vanity for the first time. They finally had become as little children, no longer "knowing" anything. He taught them for forty days before he ascended.

It is very significant that these teachings which lasted for nearly six weeks were never published. If the disciples, after three years of personal tutoring by Jesus, himself, could not "bear" them before, doubtless the world could not, even the Christian world.

So we can see that there are three major levels in the teachings of Christ: the outer teachings, the inner teachings and the hidden teachings. Then there is a fourth level of experience in which the teachings are not even taught by man. They are taught directly by the Holy Spirit. This is what the one hundred and twenty disciples first experienced on the day of Pentecost. This is as Jesus had promised at the Last Supper when he said, "When he, the Spirit of Truth, is come, he will guide you unto all truth."[2] John also described this direct level as follows: "The anointing which ye have received of him abideth in you, and YE NEED NOT THAT ANY MAN TEACH YOU, but as the same anointing teacheth you of all things and is truth and is no lie and even as it hath taught you, ye shall abide in him."[3]

The four levels might be listed as follows:

1. The Outer Truth

    Experienced by *obedience* to the literal commandments of Jesus Christ.

2. The Inner Truth

    Experienced by *faith* through the miraculous power of Jesus Christ.

3. The Hidden Truth

    Experienced by *understanding* the full meaning of Jesus Christ.

4. The Spirit of Truth or Anointing

    Experienced by being *agape-love,* the Kingdom of Heaven.

Each level has value to the person on that level and can prepare the individual for the next level toward transformation. However it is usual that most people get caught along the way, convinced that they have finally learned and experienced ALL the truth. One reason for this is semantics. The same words are used with very different meanings for each of the four levels. Each level speaks of "truth," "obedience," "commandments," "faith," "repentance," "born again," "light," "Christ," "love," "forgiveness," "sin," "Kingdom of Heaven," and many others. Each level of meaning can look like the only meaning.

As an example, take the simple word "run." It can mean a track, an engine functioning, managing, a snag in a stocking or a person going faster than a walk. No one definition is right or wrong, in and of itself. It is either appropriate or inappropriate, meaning that it works or it does not work.

In the same way the word truth has many levels of meaning. When Jesus said, "Ye shall know the truth and the truth shall make you free," it means a different concept to each level.

1. Obedience or Outer Level

    Truth means the laws and order of the Kingdom of God.

2. Faith or Inner Level

    Truth means the indwelling power of Jesus Christ, who said, "I am the truth and the life."

3. Understanding or Hidden Level

    Truth means what is

4. The Being or Transformation Level

    Truth is intention

We are not suggesting that one of these levels is better than the others. Each is perfect in its time and place. Just as Christ found it necessary in working with his special students, each of us must take the truth a step at a time. Although Jesus seemed to have no quarrel with the process of teaching with material that had hidden meanings, his disciples often found it disturbing. They asked him directly, "Why speakest thou unto them in parables?" In other words, why don't you tell them straight out, like you are doing with us? His answer was, "Because it is given unto you to know the *mysteries* of the Kingdom of Heaven, but to them IT IS NOT GIVEN. For whosoever hath, to him shall be given, and he shall have more abundance; but whosoever hath not, from him shall be taken away even that he hath. Therefore speak I to them in parables, because they seeing see not and hearing they hear not, neither do they understand."[4]

We might ask, then, why did the great multitudes follow him? The answer is because they thought they did understand him and found they were inspired and changed by what they heard him teach. These people were accustomed to living by God's rules and regulations. Jesus did not contradict their old commandments. He just carried them further. He led them past the law of outward acts to inward purity. The professionals, the scribes and Pharisees, were appalled at his "improvements," yet the people loved them, even though they went no further.

The same is true to this day. Out of several thousand followers of Christ, there may be no more than a hundred or so who will move past the first level to the second. Out of these there may not be more than a dozen or two who will go on to the third level. Out of these there may be few, if any, who will go on to the fourth. Actually, from all indications, true Christ-beings became rare in Christendom after the first generation following the time of the Savior. As a result, western civilization advanced very slowly in spiritual ways. Yet it may be in our present era of cultural change and a searching for deeper meaning that this full measure of Christian experience may return in abundance.

Just as "wise men from the East" had anticipated, and had come to welcome, the Prince of Peace two thousand years ago, Eastern teachers also recorded a prophecy nearly a thousand years ago which says that the knowledge of full enlightenment would return to the West "when iron birds fly and horses have wheels." If that is the case, this wonderful day will have much for which to thank the intervening generations of devoted believers who performed well with the knowledge they possessed. This may have been what Jesus had in mind when he said that in his Father's house were many mansions.

---

1. John 16:12 & 25
2. John 16:13
3. 1 John 2:27
4. Matt. 13:10-13

CHAPTER 4

The Carnal and the Spiritual Man

There are frequent references in the New Testament to two entirely different kinds of human beings. All of us start out in the first category, called the natural or carnal man. Christ taught that it is possible for us to die to this level of existence and to be reborn on another level called the spiritual man. Most people who are devout Christians assume that they have been "born again." I have no desire to challenge the way anyone experiences his own spirituality nor to downgrade any level of attainment. What I want to do in this chapter is to show how the scriptures describe the underlying differences in these two states of being and the level of teachings which go with each.

Possibly the easiest way to make this difference as clear as I can is to recall the story of Adam and Eve in the Garden of Eden. They were created in a place where everything was provided for them. There was no sorrow, sin or death. Neither was there joy; just peaceful existence. They were invited to tend the garden and were free to partake of the fruit of all the trees, including the one which was in the middle of the garden called the Tree of Life. The only exception to this freedom was a particular tree called the Tree of Knowledge of Good and Evil. They were carefully warned that to touch the tree or eat its fruit would mean a form of separation called death. They did partake and were driven out of the garden so that they could not eat from the Tree of Life. The way was guarded by "a flaming sword which turned every way."

21

Whether one accepts this story as literal history or as a mythological legend is not the point with which I want to deal. The real significance of this story is that it is an absolutely perfect description of how you and I came into this world. You might ask how is that? Well, were we not all created by Life in a garden-like paradise called the womb where there was no sorrow, sin or fear of death? Neither was there joy; just peaceful existence. We were freely partaking of a total union with life, which we might call the Tree of Life. Then, in the process of being born, with its pain and disturbing shocks, we had what they call in est a "number one" experience. Our minds, like an over-worked computer, went to work in the name of survival to compare what was happening out here, now, with that "serene" state we had before in the womb. It programmed itself to judge everything which made us feel bad as a threat to be resisted—called evil. Everything which made us feel nice and comfortable was to be desired as good. Therefore, would we not say that we had partaken of the fruit called a "knowledge of good and evil?" As infants, we were sure that what was painful was bad and what was pleasant was good. Since everything in life is or could become disturbing, the world around us was gradually sensed as a very threatening place. Constantly we had to be on guard.

That was it! In leaving our "Garden of Eden," we gave up our unity with creation and faced a strange, new world with an agitated, see-saw mind. In scrip-tures it is called a double mind. I am not insinuating that this was bad or unnecessary. My point is to remind us that the entire content and purpose of the mind in its function of survival is to perfect its knowledge of what is "good" and what is "evil." In the womb we evidently experienced none of this. Life or Spirit was for Go. The mind is a Go/Not Go machine, just like a computer. The mind is never single since it is continually testing between what is good/evil, right/wrong, safe/unsafe, nice/bad, mine/yours, what is/what ought to be, and the best/worst. So we see the similarity to Adam and Eve. Adam would correspond to our intellect, Eve to the emotions, which partook first. In coming out of the garden each of us ate of the forbidden fruit and died to the Tree of Life, the union with Spirit.

If you want to see how totally we are committed to the Tree of Death, try to visualize existing without a definite knowledge of good and evil. That discriminating mental capacity we have nurtured and, yes, worshipped, is our most prized of all our possessions. What do we really value most, in the final analysis? Is it not our knowledge, our beliefs, as to what is really good and what is really bad? Isn't that what we feel makes us a person of some worth, why we honor our good name? Is there any way we can ever be angry except when something is not the way we KNOW it should be? Do we ever feel gratification except when things are the way we KNOW they should be? For example, why does one read this book? Isn't it to increase one's knowledge of good and evil? Our mind is constantly screening the ideas expressed here to make sure that it does not take false for being true.

Now, remember, although this good/bad mentality is the only existence most of us have experienced and also there are all kinds of ways to make it better, there is no way the mind of the knowledge of good and evil can become one with the Spirit. Spirit is infinitely total. The double mind cannot co-exist with the Tree of Life. The flaming sword of truth, which turns EVERY WAY, is a two edged sword, exposing both sides of our feelings—hate and guilt. We hate (we say resent, dislike, can't stand) what is not good in others. We have guilt (we say regret, depression, anxiety) about what we see as not good in ourselves. Hate is division, that which pushes us away, tends to separate us from others. Love is union, that which draws us together. The very division we experience between the "me" and the "not me," "us" and "them," is rooted in fear, the true emotion of hate and guilt. The Tree of Life is the Tree of Love, love without fear.

If there is no hope for the perfection and reunification of the mind, what is the way? We have said that the nature of enlightenment is to discover or experience who we are. Since we are convinced that we are our thinking mind and the sensing body, attempts at self-discovery or self-knowing with the mind have turned out to be little more than self-analysis. Although self-criticism may enable us to get better, it never produces a true conversion. Conversion does not really mean agreement to some belief system. It means to turn about, to con-vert, 180 degrees. Instead of being taken in by the mind, we see the mind for what it is. We see that it is not the real self. This realization is called CONFESSION. As we give up trusting the mind to "put humpty-dumpty back together again," we experience the spiritual state called SURRENDER.

Conversion (confession and surrender) is not transformation. It is preparatory and enables us to effectively work with the hidden teachings which lead to transformation. We are converted—away from trusting ourselves as the mind—to being a disidentifying observer who watches the fascinating activity of the double mind.

The first two levels of truth, the outer and inner teachings, are addressed to the natural man. As these teachings are accepted by the mind, the heavy burden of greed and pride are lightened considerably. The outer teachings are designed to lift the mind to a higher sense of good and evil. The inner teachings enable the mind to realize that there is infinite power and goodness available to man through faith in something outside of himself. While the mind improves by being more "spiritual" and "good," it claims to have reason to congratulate itself. It becomes proud of its humility. As Paul says, "For they, being ignorant of God's righteousness (perfect union and agape) and going about to establish their own righteousness (being right) have not submitted (turned around, converted) themselves unto the righteousness of God."[1]

Of course, the self does not want to disidentify with the mind because to do so would mean death to the artificial union which makes up the natural man. It appears to us that without that identity there would be no "self," for that is all we think the self really is. About the only way this separation can take place is by some devastating experience which reveals the mind for the unreliable idiot it really is. This humiliation is often referred to in the wisdom schools as the initiation, where one goes through the "third degree."

At this point, when the student discovers that he is not the mind nor the body, he is called an initiate, a true beginner on the way. Now he is able to receive and "bear" the awesome simplicity of the hidden teachings. Suddenly he begins to see the outer and inner teachings in a completely new light. He sees that he was really told it ALL, all the time. After considerable work at the third level, he MAY experience transformation. Then, and not until then, will he truly know who and what he is. This is called the anointing of light, a new level of being in which one experiences eternal life, being perfect in love. This is the spiritual man.

In the light of what we have just discussed, notice the depth of meaning in this familiar statement of Christ when he said, "The light (understanding) of the body is the eye (way we perceive things, our point of view), if therefore thine eye be SINGLE, thy whole body shall be full of LIGHT (true understanding—agape). But if thine eye be evil (seeing with fear), thy whole body shall be full of darkness (misconceptions, illusions), If therefore the light that is in thee be darkness, HOW GREAT IS THAT DARKNESS!"[2]

Paul put it another way, "For they that are after the flesh (identify with the mind and the body) do mind the things of the flesh, but they that are after the Spirit the things of the Spirit. For to be carnally minded is death (separation from directly experiencing Life), but to be spiritually minded is life and peace, because the CARNAL MIND IS ENMITY AGAINST GOD (Unity of Being); for it is not subject to the law of God (agape, union), neither indeed can be."[3]

It is said that the natural man is carnal, sensual and devilish. Our minds have such depraved definitions for these words that we feel that such adjectives certainly do not apply to us. Let us take another look. Are not the following definitions descriptive of all of us?

CARNAL   desiring the comforts and approval of the world and/or heaven.

SENSUAL   desiring to have pleasure and escape embarrassment.

DEVILISH   desiring to control others and not be controlled.

By reading the epistles in the New Testament, it is evident that although some individuals experienced transformation, the majority got caught up on the first or second levels. For this reason the hidden teachings never became the open teachings even in that highly blessed generation. We can find frequent scriptural references to the existence of such hidden knowledge, called the mysteries of godliness, yet it is never openly spelled out. All of the writers, including James, Peter, John and especially Paul, chastised those who were "called to be saints" for their inability to bear the true mysteries and "wisdom of God." Paul called these teachings the MEAT, the real substance of the gospel.

All Paul could give them openly was what he called the MILK. His letter to the squabbling church at Corinth is a prime example. He reminded them that even though they were enjoying great gifts, such as tongues, prophesying, revelations, healings and so forth, they were divided by contentions, jealousies, diverse doctrines and fragmented loyalties.

Paul explained, "And I, brethren, *could not* speak unto you as unto spiritual, but as unto carnal, even as

unto *babes in Christ*. I have fed you with milk and
not with meat, for hitherto ye were *not able to bear
it*. NEITHER YET NOW ARE YE ABLE. For ye
are yet carnal, for whereas there is among you envy-
ing and strife and division; are ye not CARNAL
AND WALK AS (natural) MEN.''[4] Then Paul went
on to discuss what many have mistakenly understood
to be the deepest aspects of Christianity, such as
faith, spiritual gifts, resurrection, love, unity of the
church, morality and the sacraments. Yet by Paul's
clear declaration, these are all the milk.

The Corinthians were not the only ones, of course.
In his general letter to all Hebrew (Jewish) Christians, Paul wrote: '' . . . seeing ye are dull of hearing
. . . ye have need that one teach you again which be
the first principles of the oracles of God and are
become such as have need of MILK and not of strong
MEAT.''[5] Then he goes on to discuss with them such
''milk'' as the redeeming power of Christ, the nature
of faith, the holiness of the priesthood of God, enter-
ing into his rest, privileges and blessings of the new
covenant and rejoicing under the cross.

The milk of truth (first and second levels) is designed for the benefit of carnal man. By the teachings
of these levels we can begin to discover many of the
illusions and misconceptions which keep our double
minds bound so tightly to judging good and evil,
having needs, blaming, justifying, pride and vanity.
These are called the chains of hell for out of them
come all the misery and anxiety of our carnal lives.
Some of the chains are broken when a person discovers that even his own standards of good and evil
totally condemn him, putting him completely at the
mercy of God. ''All have sinned and come short of

the glory of God." This is man's first step in moving away from the Tree of Knowledge.

The second step on the milk level is when he begins to see that in spite of his "evil and carnal state," the Father's love for him is so great that he sent his only begotten Son to pay the price, clean the slate, justify him before the eternal balance so that he is free from blame. In this step, he can begin to release some of that deep, hidden guilt and feelings of inferiority held in the mind of the knowledge of good and evil.

Then the third step on the milk level is for him to "do unto others as was done to him," by forgiving and accepting his enemies as he has been able to forgive and accept himself.

You may have noticed that this wonderful milk of the gospel still deals with a knowledge of good and evil. However, it is working like yeast, lightening the burden of it so that life can be much sweeter.

Paul yearned to be able to work on the deeper level with the people who were yet such babes in Christ. He acknowledged that such spiritual treasures were discussed only among those who were enlightened. The way he described this to the Corinthians is very revealing. He said, "Howbeit we speak *wisdom* among them that are PERFECT; yet not the wisdom of this world . . . that come to nought, but we speak the wisdom of God in a mystery, even THE HIDDEN WISDOM, which God ordained before the world unto our glory . . . Now we have received, not the spirit of the world (knowledge of good and evil), but the spirit which is of God, that we might know the things that are freely given to us of God."[6]

Notice that Paul dares to mention that there were those who were "perfect." That is very much worth noting. In effect he is saying that there were some among them who followed Jesus' command "to be ye therefore PERFECT." As we have already mentioned, that word is out of reach for any of us who identify with the mind. To a double mind there is absolutely no possible comprehension of anybody, except Christ, being perfect. To us, perfect means TOTALLY IDEAL, having absolutely nothing that is less than ideal. To the mind, everyone can have some good and certainly has some not-so-good. The "eye," not being single, sees good and evil, thus is filled with darkness.

During Christ's ministry, the disciples were even judgmental of Jesus. At the time of the crucifixion, this darkness of judging reached its climax in total self-rejection when they failed to fulfill their own ideals of what a good disciple was supposed to be. Then suddenly, with the return of the master and his greater and clearer teachings, they discovered for themselves that everything and everybody is actually a perfect part of a perfect whole, created exactly the way they are, doing exactly the things they do. Thus the eye, instead of trying to second-guess everything with "if this, then that," suddenly becomes single and "the whole body is filled with light."

Once a person has been enlightened, seeing that he is not the mind but is a function of divine essence which is the observer of the mind and body, real work can commence. At this point, the true, real self, having just been brought back from the dead, is still only a very tiny infant. The spiritual man is but a child. A whole new world is being experienced. Everything seems so different than it was before, even though it is all really the same. As they say in est, the content has not been changed. It is the ability to experience the contents that has been totally transformed.

The teaching of the spiritual man is called the fulness of TRUTH, the meat. The basic and elementary portion of this hidden wisdom is taught initiates by one who has it. The greater portion can only be given directly by the Spirit of Truth, Life itself. Paul describes the awesome magnitude of this experience in a letter to the church at Ephesus: "Whereby, when ye read, ye may understand my KNOWLEDGE IN THE MYSTERY OF CHRIST, which in other ages was not made known unto the sons of men, as it is now revealed unto his holy apostles and prophets by the Spirit . . . that he would grant you, according to the RICHES OF HIS GLORY, to be strengthened with might by his Spirit in the inner man (the true self), that CHRIST MAY DWELL IN YOUR HEARTS BY FAITH, that ye being rooted and grounded in LOVE (agape), may be able to COMPREHEND with all saints what is THE BREADTH, AND LENGTH, AND DEPTH AND HEIGHT, and to KNOW THE LOVE OF CHRIST *which passeth knowledge* (of good and evil), that ye might be filled with ALL THE FULNESS OF GOD."[7]

1. Romans 10:3
2. Matt. 6:21-23
3. Romans 8:5-9
4. I Cor. 3:1-3
5. Heb. 3:11-12
6. I Cor. 2:6-7 & 12
7. Eph. 3:4-5 & 16-19

CHAPTER 5
Notions and Beliefs

In these last several chapters we have looked at some very significant ideas about Christianity. We have talked about truth being on four different levels and about two totally different levels of existence, one with a double mind nourished by milk and the other with the single mind nourished by meat. We have talked about conversion and transformation. It is difficult for us to read such material without testing it in our minds—is it true or false, right or wrong? In dealing with a significant subject, we want to be sure we form the correct conclusions to be very certain about things. We have considered our knowledge of certainty—our beliefs—to be a highly valued prize gained from our studies and experience.

The New Testament talks a lot about the value of believing. I would like you to set to one side your views on those scriptures for the time being because we will deal with the subject later. I will only mention that what the New Testament is referring to in the word "believe" might be something totally different than what we usually understand it to be.

In the next few chapters we will deal with some ideas put out by est. We have mentioned that est is not a religion nor a set of beliefs. However, many graduates of est have probably taken the data and made beliefs. In fact, Werner wrote recently that the greatest problem est has at the present time is that so many of the graduates "believe" in est. What a paradox.

So before I go on to the next chapters, I thought it would be appropriate to talk about "certainty" in three categories: beliefs, notions, and knowing.

In the est training the first chalk-talk is on the subject of certainty. My comments on the subject are in line with the est material, although I am touching only a few of the points they cover.

Ordinarily, we are sure we know what we experience. So if I am walking in the forest at twilight and think I see a grizzly bear up the trail, I say that I know the bear is there. Yet it may turn out to be a stump. So what I really know is that I experienced the sensations of there being a bear. That is the fact. Based upon the experience, I act. I can either fight, freeze or run. If I am armed and interested in sticking around to check on my experience, I may find out there is no bear after all. As I get within a few feet of the spot, I experience it as a tree stump. Then on touching it, I experience it as a fabricated tree stump built as a prop for the movie being filmed on the site.

At each step of the process, the mind wants to take the experience and form fixed, definite conclusions. We call these our beliefs. As est puts it, beliefs represent a very low level of certainty. This is not to say that beliefs are bad. I doubt whether we could function without a whole pack of beliefs. We just want to remember that we assume our beliefs are a high level of certainty when actually they are not.

In the est training, the trainees are asked not to believe or disbelieve any of the data presented. They are asked to just listen to what is presented and get in touch with their experience of the data as a possible point of view. That is very difficult for most of us.

Our double mind wants to establish the truth or error
of every idea we hear—that is its survival game of
being right. So what est is asking us to do is balance
the data in the middle.

So what do we call something that we hold in the
middle? We can call it a notion. est does not claim to
present any conclusions or beliefs, AND it looks to
most people like est is presenting NOTHING EX-
CEPT conclusions and beliefs. The reason is that
most of us are so very unfamiliar with notions that we
make conclusions and beliefs out of them. We assume
everyone else is doing the same.

What is a notion? A notion is an idea which is not
held as a conclusion. In the example of the bear, I
knew I experienced a sensation of being near a bear.
This was a fact. Since I have previously found appearances to be very deceiving in twilight, I could
recognize that whether there is a bear there or not has
not yet been completely established. So I need not
make a conclusion. I hold the idea as a notion, a real
possibility.

If I function from the "belief" that there is a bear
in fact, I will start running and not stop for a mile,
yelling all the way. If I function from the notion, I
can take precautionary action while constantly check-
ing out the facts. Beliefs lock us in. Notions allow
greater flexibility, remaining open for additional information. Notions are held squarely in the middle of
the awareness.

You might notice that the middle is ALWAYS
SINGLE. There are no two middles, only two sides.
This may be the only way to have an "eye that is
single." At least that is a notion we can have about it.
By not making a conclusion about an experience, we

are free to hold the idea as an interesting point of view and EXAMINE OUR EXPERIENCE WITH THE IDEA. Whatever happens in such an experience just happens. The mind wants to take the results of an experiment and move the notion from neutral to a conclusion so we can say, "Now I understand."

To conclude means to end, finish and get done. That which is finished is closed, dead. Aliveness is open-ended, curious, flexible and spontaneous. Conclusions are stuck, fixed, all tied up. We can even make a conclusion that all beliefs are conclusions or we can hold it as a notion, just examining our experience with the point of view. The results with a certain notion may be very consistent and we may have a fairly high degree of certainty. Yet, since it is still a notion, we are open to something that comes along which may not fit the idea.

We usually form conclusions by a mental process called logic. Logic appears so logical. However, on close examination it is hardly what it claims to be. Logic says that "if this is so," then "that is so." If A, then B. Logic says that if I saw a bear, there was a bear. However, although my experience of the sensation of the bear is a fact, the actual presence of a bear is an assumption. Logic starts with an assumption and ends with a conclusion. Every belief we have starts with at least one assumption.

Let us take the example of the last two chapters. To most people it would appear that I was presenting a lot of conclusions—beliefs. Actually, those were all notions of mine. They are ideas which I do not disbelieve and neither do I believe. In order for me to believe them—logically—what are some of the assumptions I would have to take as fully established facts? There would be an assumption that the Bible was originally a totally accurate record of accurate memories of actual events which were accurately understood. Also, that the King James translation was an accurate translation of the Greek manuscripts which were accurate copies of the original manuscripts. On top of that, I would have to assume that the way I understand the English words is the same understanding intended in the original Aramaic spoken by the people involved. That is just the beginning of the assumptions. How in the world can we be satisfied to make conclusions out of all that?

Actually, once a person understands how beautifully notions work in one's life, there is NO NEED to make beliefs out of them. There is not one advantage that I have found in going beyond a notion. There can be many disadvantages, however. For example, those ideas of the Gospel will not work if they are believed. The eye that is single does not come out of conclusions, it comes out of directly experiencing experiences. Beliefs keep us stuck in the mind where we do not experience experience, we conceptualize experience. In other words, we experience the concepts about the experience, not the experience itself. Non-experiencing experience is a separation from living. In the scriptures this is called sleep and death. Christ said to awake, rise from the dead.

Notions allow us to examine our experience of a point of view to see whether it contributes to our aliveness. If it does, it does. If it doesn't, it doesn't. That is all we are knowing. To assume more, to speculate and to create explanations become our barriers to aliveness—unless those are merely notions as well.

We have all been told that experience is the best teacher. This is another belief. How about a different idea. Experience is all there is! Experience is not a teacher, it is what living is. Where there is no direct experiencing, there is no aliveness. Instead of accepting aliveness, we want to prove things by our experience so we can be right and safe.

When I was a total believer in my particular denomination, our oldest daughter was diagnosed as having polyps in her lower intestine, plainly visible on x-ray photographs. An operation was recommended as the only possible solution. We followed the biblical injunction. Our family fasted and those holding the priesthood anointed her with oil and blessed her. The recovery was immediate. What joy! What proof! From this miraculous experience, I knew even more than before that we had the right faith, were in the right church, with the right priesthood, with the right ordinances, with the right understanding of divinity. My beliefs were confirmed? If she had not been healed, then I would have blamed it on our not having enough faith or it was just not the will of God. It is our beliefs in God we worship—not God.

Another example might be of interest at this point. A civil engineer in England, George De La Warr, was running some way-out experiments on "radiating" soil to increase plant productivity. The results obtained by him and his wife were very convincing. To extend their evidence, they asked a nationally known plant-breeding firm to have their workers plant seeds in some treated and untreated soils. The resulting difference was negligible. De La Warr was not discouraged because he had been working with a notion that there might be a human element in the tests. So he had the growers repeat the experiment.

This time he showed the workers which section of the soil had been radiated. The increased growth in the treated soil was remarkable. What De La Warr had not revealed, however, was that on the second test NONE of the soil had been treated. He had established evidence to support the surprising notion that the mental attitude of people involved was the major element rather than his fancy black boxes.[1]

Few people realize the capability of the mind to create real experiences to support what is believed. This faculty can range from the way the mind interprets experiences to its amazing ability to affect results. In between these two poles is the ability of the mind to create its own experiences which are only inside the mind.

We have all seen hypnotism produce amazing experiences for the people involved. Actually, what the hypnotist does is to over-ride the "Not Go" part of the double mind. We have been told that a person cannot be induced to do an immoral act under hypnosis which he would not do ordinarily—such as to kill someone. However all the hypnotist has to do is tell the subject that the intended victim has just killed someone and is going to kill again unless the subject shoots him first. With such false information as justification, the trigger will be pulled.

Under hypnosis, the subject BELIEVES. There are no notions. The hypnotist has made a single mind out of half of the double mind and the ability of such a mind is absolutely amazing. The subject can make his body so rigid that a two hundred pound weight can rest on his stomach while his body is suspended between two chairs. He can be handed an onion and told that it is an apple. The "apple" is enjoyed, with no watering of the eyes and no burning of the mouth.

A person can be touched with ice and told that it is a very hot poker. A large blister will form where contact is made.

Since most hypnotists first put their subjects into a sleeping trance, it may be difficult for us to equate such experiences with anything which happens to us in a waking state. Kreskin, a successful hypnotist of international fame, after hypnotizing an estimated 35,000 people, discovered that he could achieve the same manifestations with the subject wide awake.

He reports one of many examples in a chapter called "The Power of Suggestion."

> On occasion I'll carry what looks like a dozen pairs of eyeglasses on stage, and in setting up the demonstration, point out that these particular "glasses" will cause great distortion, so that the subjects will see one another as though looking into "fun-house" mirrors at carnivals. After I place the "glasses" on their foreheads, asking them please not to touch them, the subjects look at one another and begin to break up. It is interesting to observe how they handle this suggestion. Some claim the others have the heads of giraffes, eyes like headlights or noses like bananas. They are remembering what they have seen in similar true distortions. On completing the test, I stick a finger through the frames, showing both the subjects and the audience that there are no lenses.[2]

Another example Kreskin described had to do with producing an experience to support the induced "belief" in flying saucers.

> Dr. Jay Allan Hynek, professor of astronomy at Northwestern University . . . contacted me about this area of suggestibility phenomenon . . . I agreed that a small percentage of the sightings (of UFO's) might possibly be explained, or could be identified, in psychological terms, and offered to "stage" a sighting for his observation. He came up to TV station CJOH in Ottawa, where I tape my syndicated show, on a selected night.

Conditioning fourteen subjects, I told them that when we went to "black" for the commercial, they would return to the audience, dress warmly and then proceed outside the studio. Cameras had been set up outdoors, one of which would monitor the demonstration for the studio audience. I assured the subjects that when I came out and dropped a handkerchief, they would see three flying objects. Assisting in the test was the news director Max Keeping from CJOH. His job was to interview the subjects, on camera, before and during the "sighting."

Along with Hynek and the studio audience, I watched the subjects as we went to black for the commercial break. They dutifully returned to their seats, collected coats and gloves and then filed out into the night where Keeping was waiting. He began to question them about UFO's and most expressed great skepticism.

I watched for a moment and then went outdoors to join them, Dr. Hynek following. The night was clear, icy cold. Stars were out. Mingling with them near the reporter, I pulled out the handkerchief, wiped my forehead with it and then dropped it. In a few seconds the fourteen subjects were sighting three flying saucers, pointing up and discussing them with Keeping. Skepticism had vanished.

One man rushed back into the studio, asking permission to use the phone to report UFO's. Studio personnel, briefed on what was occurring, refused his request. He returned outside, bitterly denouncing the studio employees for their apathy.

I then said, in a loud voice, that it appeared to me that one of the saucers was descending and that it would probably hover over the station within a few minutes. Two of the subjects began running across the snowy field toward the highway. I yelled, "Release," and they turned back: the other twelve subjects responded to the same signal.

Keeping began asking them about the saucers. Uniformly, the subjects either laughed at him or questioned his sanity. No one had seen "flying saucers."

Dr. Hynek was very interested to know exactly what they had seen. We all returned inside, out of subfreezing weather, and I suggested the fourteen subjects back into their imaginative mental discovery. They responded in considerable detail including descriptions of shapes and designs of the UFO's. The colors varied; some saw yellow saucers and some saw green. Notably, no subject saw more than three saucers, the exact number I had suggested.[2]

These people were not lying. They were telling the TRUTH of their experience, which was ALL inside the mind. The only reality we really know is what we believe we experience. However, the mind does not want to stop with the experience. It tries to explain the cause, significance and meaning of the experience.

I will give a common example of how we extend our own experience. Let us assume that I am asked to test some punch for sweetness. I do so just after eating some cake. The punch tastes sour to me. I therefore declare, flatly, "The punch IS sour." Another person comes along who has been sucking on a lemon. His experience is that the punch is too sweet. The punch is what it is. Both of us have formed beliefs about what the punch is. We would be more accurate to realize that all we know is our experience and we have only a notion about the punch, itself.

Another example, if you have a warm, burning sensation in your chest, that is your experience. This you KNOW. It is not a notion nor a belief. It is an experience. You can describe it accurately. Anything beyond that, however, is not knowledge. You may identify it as the Spirit of the Lord, love, anxiety or heart burn. The truth of the matter might be any one of these, or some other, such as suggestion. The point is that the experience is fact. We know facts. We believe explanations.

I once had a good friend who wanted to fast

twenty-one days to receive a revelation from God about what he was to do with his life. The twenty-first day was a Sunday. Nothing had taken place so he continued in prayer all that night. Just at the first morning light, a man walked through the dining room door into the kitchen where he was. The person was dressed strangely and began to speak earnestly to him in some foreign language. As my friend realized that the answer was coming in an incomprehensible form, he hit the table with his clenched fists and cried, "Oh, God, why cannot I understand?" In that instant he could understand every word.

The messenger showed him a vision of the whole world and how destruction and pestilence would devastate the inhabitants before the end of the sixth year from that date. He was told what he was to do and shown a number of things which he did not understand at the time (though he received understanding of them later). Then the visitor turned and went out of the room.

My friend was ecstatic. He was walking on clouds for weeks. Not only had his prayers been answered but he knew the future, had his religious views confirmed, felt totally anointed by the Lord and on and on. That vision occurred in 1959. As for my friend, he assured me it was a real experience—the most vivid, awesome event ever to happen to him. Yet what was it? Was it a visitation of an angel of God, the devil, his imagination? How would anyone ever know? It was his experience. The fact that all those predictions failed to come to pass in six years was also something he experienced.

Now for me, I did not have the experience, so I do not even know that the event occurred. What I do know for sure is that in 1969 I had the experience of him telling me about it in great, solemn detail. That I know. Beyond this experience, I do not know.

What our minds have been doing most of our lives is to go further. The mind makes explanations which are accepted as the TRUTH. Out of our explanations we form our needs of how to get what "ought to be." Our beliefs about what ought to be are our barriers to aliveness. Aliveness is to directly experience what is, this moment. Since the mind thinks that "what is" is not as good as "more, better and/or different," we are always comparing "what is" with "what if that." So we experience a busy mind which is analyzing, comparing, remembering, categorizing and what not. All of this comes from the great value we put on the adored belief system of the double mind.

To review, a notion is an idea, an explanation or description, which is not accepted or rejected as fact. It is never a conclusion nor a belief. It is a point of view which may be experimented with to see what we experience. Whatever the experience, it is never proof. We never need to stabilize a notion into a belief. Everything we can do constructively with a belief we can also do with a notion.

As we see the grand and hilarious joke of our great investment in always being right, we can upgrade our beliefs to a much higher degree of certainty called, "I see that I do not totally see." It may turn out that beyond this is a state of aliveness called NATURAL KNOWING. This is another notion of est.

---

1. The Secret Life of Plants, Peter Tompkins and Christopher Bird, pp. 355-358

2. From The Amazing World of Kreskin, by Kreskin. Copyright 1973 by Kreskin. Pages 110, 112–114. Reprinted by permission of Random House, Inc.

CHAPTER 6

The Notion of Transformation

Werner Erhard says that transformation of the self is beyond ordinary understanding. If it cannot be understood, then shall we spend a chapter explaining it? No, not really. Yet, we would like to understand why it cannot be understood.

If we stop to think a moment, we should not be surprised. Let us take something as ordinary as our sight. Can we understand seeing? Could we really explain it to someone who has never seen? We recognize when we are seeing and when we are not, yet we cannot even understand how the mind makes seeing work. Our medical specialists understand some of the relationships involved in seeing but not seeing itself. The same is true of all our hundreds of senses because the mind is something that works for us even if we do not understand it.

One of the best examples we find in nature is the transformation of a caterpillar into a butterfly. Is there any way that the spiny, multi-ped worm could ever get the least understanding of what is on the other side of that crazy cocoon it is building? In fact, even man cannot understand how the caterpillar's program works. We could study a butterfly in isolation for a thousand years and never guess that these colorful, flitting insects are the same individuals that used to be such amazing worms.

Transformation means to be totally different. Two gases, hydrogen and oxygen, give no indication in their characteristics as separate elements as to what the water into which they can be transformed will be like. One of the closest words might be transubstantiation which is used to describe the transformation of bread into flesh, a doctrine of the Catholic communion. It is the idea of one substance coming through another.

Before we discuss the transformation of self, let us start with a transformation of the way we see the universe. Science has been making vast strides in getting deeper and deeper into the characteristics of physical reality. All kinds of beliefs have been painfully discarded along the way as new theories were established as facts. In all of this research, the most fascinating and perplexing has been the origin and development of life. Evolution, through survival of the fittest, became a prominent theory since there is much evidence showing that life-forms have never ceased to evolve. Yet there are many unanswerable questions of almost insurmountable magnitude. Life-forms demonstrate an infinite magnitude of order and balance. Where did this come from? Out of disorder and chaos? Science has yet to create one demonstration where anything goes from disorder to order. It is always the other way around. So how did all this happen?

It is very possible that science has got the cart before the horse. They have made the general assumption that matter-energy is eternal. It cannot be created nor can it be destroyed; it can only be changed. None is lost, none is gained. In contrast, life appears to come and go, like waves of the ocean. Life seems to be only matter in complex motion. So what most science has been looking for is how eternal matter created the temporary manifestations of living organisms. Also, since the material universe functions as a great machine, it is believed that life is also just another machine, even though of exotic order.

Now, let us totally reverse this whole approach. What if it is life that is eternal and matter which is temporary? Instead of the universe producing life, life has created the material universe. This is not as ridiculous or unscientific as it may sound. You must remember that our scientists have established that the way we see matter is an illusion. That hard stuff we take for granted is actually very ethereal. Your hands that are holding this book, the chair you are sitting on, the floor and walls around you, all seem so solid, practical and non-mystical. Yet our laboratories have found that all these are almost totally space. For example, think of just one atom that is spinning in the period at the end of this sentence. Yes, right there. Think of one of the millions of atoms in the ink that made the dot. If we were to enlarge the nucleus of that atom to the size of an average orange, the electrons circling around it would be approximately four hundred miles away, with nothing but space in between. No other atoms are in there. And what is the nucleus? It is a universe in itself and is mostly space. Ultimately, we find all of these particles turn out to be no more than energy charges.

Science tells us we live in a "reality" that has no straight lines, no solids, no surfaces and is only energy. What would life be, then? How would we know? That is like asking the fish to tell us what water is. However, we could take the notion that one characteristic of life is that of being the initiator. In the Bible it is called Creator. In est it is called source or cause. Source is! Everything else is effect!

As present day scientists ponder these ever more awesome discoveries about what we call reality, some are beginning to talk like a great scientist that I heard recently. He is a man of impeccable credentials and is head of one of our most respected research institutions. He thoughtfully declared, "The more we discover about the universe, the less and less it looks like a great machine and the more and more it looks like a great thought." He went on to speak about something they are calling consciousness in the same way spiritual leaders often speak of the Creator. He said it appears that our highest function is participation in consciousness.

Well, now! That is a whole new ball game. It is quite a notion. With life producing the universe, then life-forms are localized vortexes of the indivisible source. Although effect is multiple, source would be singular. Source creates the chain-reaction of effect, effect, effect, effect, etc. Although each effect looks like the cause of the next effect, it is "false cause," being only the effect of other effects. This leads ultimately back to the source of the whole. This is another notion of est.

Change always has to do with alteration and persistence of what is. In fact, only because everything is constantly changing (electrons spinning around the nucleus, for example), do things exist at all. From what I gather, if everything in the atomic universe suddenly stopped, it would just cease to exist. So it appears that the solidness of the universe is really only compressed energy bound together by interacting polarities.

So now we come back to our major theme. What am I? Am I the body and mind which are only polarized energy complexes, functioning totally as effect? That which is source is life. So as long as I identify with effect, effect is what I will experience— totally. If I break loose from the restrictions and the illusions of that belief system, it may possibly be that the infinite aspect of being will be discovered as the real self.

Werner expressed it as follows: "It's not the self we have to give up. As a matter of fact, it's the exact opposite. It's that which we've been CALLING the self and ISN'T, which needs to be given up. Who we actually are is that self which doesn't discover the truth, or figure out the truth, but that self which KNOWS the truth. The word 'know' has also had grave damage done to it. What we normally mean by 'know' is 'remember.' Remembering is a very low level of knowing. It has, as a matter of fact, no real knowing in it at all."[1]

Let us go back to Jesus at the Last Supper for just a bit. Jesus emphasized that there was no way the disciples could BEAR the deeper truth at that time. Remember, the only way they could understand, having double minds, was to assume that everything he was telling them had to do with becoming better. What Jesus did speak about was being of total one-ness with the Father. He told them he was a manifestation of that state, yet they could not bear (comprehend) it either. So Jesus said, "If ye had known me, ye should have known my Father also and from henceforth ye know him and have seen him."

One of the disciples seemed to have understood that Jesus was talking about this oneness as being a unity of parts, like a unity of purpose between two friends. So he asked Jesus to show them the

Father—the other part. Jesus answered, "Have I been so long a time with you, and yet has thou not known me, Philip? He that hath seen me hath seen the Father . . . The words that I speak unto you, I speak not of myself, but the Father that dwelleth in me, he doeth the works. Believe me that I am in the Father and the Father in me . . . "[2]

At the conclusion of the Last Supper, Jesus prayed aloud before his disciples, asking "that they all may be one; as thou, Father art in me, and I in thee, that they also may be ONE IN US."[3]

We may have many different beliefs about what the Father is according to differing Christian doctrines, yet we would possibly all agree in the concept that the Father is total, creative presence. In other words, He is total SOURCE. Jesus was at least saying that he was consciously one with Source, that his every word and act came from Source. Thus Jesus was all there was—"the way, the truth and the life." When he referred to the disciples' own day of awakening, he said, "At that day ye shall know that I am in my Father (which is total Source), and YE IN ME AND I IN YOU."[4]

These words of Christ have inspired and also frustrated sincere believers down through the last nineteen centuries because they speak of total and complete union. It refers to a perfect union which would require that one be "perfect even as your Father in heaven is perfect." As John declared, "God is light, and in him is no darkness at all. If we say that we have fellowship with him and walk in darkness, we lie and do not the truth."[5]

So in the light of such a possible state of being, I

am going to quote from a lengthy talk Werner Erhard gave to est graduates in 1976. For the previous five years he had been the subject of notoriety and mystery as the founder of est. Many had been asking the questions: who is he, what are his motives, what is he trying to do and who does he think he is? Werner had revealed very little about himself during that time, other than to acknowledge that he had been far from perfect and had left few stones unturned in his own efforts to become "better" until he experienced transformation in 1971. Then in August, 1976, he chose to be more specific. He repeated a talk in eight different cities around the country attended by more than 20,000 est graduates. He talked about the transformation of the est organization, which is really about the transformation of self. Although we will eventually use quotations from many parts of this talk, the following is taken from his introduction.

I'm going to be sharing an experience with you. As we go along it might sound as if I'm sharing about myself, about Werner Erhard. I'm not. I'm going to be sharing something with you about the SELF, the same self that you actually are. What I'm really sharing with you is about your actual self, not your story—and not my story. Unfortunately, to do that, I'm going to have to tell you my story and I really think my story is a little boring. Yet I have no other way to do it, so I'll be telling you the story of my transformation.

About 13 years ago, I experienced in my life what is sometimes called a "transformation." It lasted for three months and then it went away. After that three-month period, I was very clear that an "untransformed" life was not worth living, and that the only intelligent thing to do with my life was to devote it to recapturing (that's the way I said it 13 years ago) that experience, whatever it was.

Now the question is, was what I experienced actually transformation? The answer is no. Because it ended, it was over—and true transformation has no end. Transformation is not something that ends, or something that starts, or that has a middle. Transformation is not an event or a thing. There is no such THING as transformation.

So here I am talking about transformation, and in almost the same breath, I tell you that there is no such thing as transformation. How do I make sense of that?

I don't make SENSE of it. And you shouldn't try to UNDERSTAND it because transformation can't be understood. It can, however, be GOTTEN. So don't try to make sense out of this. Like in the training, just let it sit on your lap, like a brick. Don't try to figure it out. Just be with it and you'll get it.

What I mean by the term "transformation" doesn't have the properties that THINGS do. No position or location, no time, no form, no beginning and no end. It doesn't look like anything. It doesn't feel like anything. And it does not happen. Transformation just IS and you can create it and you can know it. It just is, and while you can know that it is, you can't perceive it or sense it or feel it.

To explain it (and it can't really be explained), you could say that transformation is a shift in the definition or locus of self from content to context, from identifying one's self as point of view, story, personality, body, and so on, to recognizing one's self as the context in which all things occur. It's not an event; it's a context for events to occur in—a space.

That's what transformation is—and that is not at all what happened 13 years ago, which was a special event, or, to use Abraham Maslow's term, a peak experience.

A lot of people have misunderstood est and thought that est is a peak experience. I think peak experiences are terrific, and the human potential movement, which is a great thing, is about peak experiences. But est is not a peak experience. est is about transformation.

Ordinarily, life consists of CONCEPTUALIZING your experience. A peak experience consists of EXPERIENCING your experience directly. What happened to me 13 years ago was that I had a special kind of experienced experience—it was direct experience of SELF. While that's great, it was an event, not true transformation. What happens in transformation is that your self IS, not your self "is now but wasn't before." In transformation the self just IS.

You see, transformation transcends the laws of things and events. Transformation is actually a miracle. It transcends the limits of time. Everybody's been told there's nothing you can do about the past. Not so. The truth of the matter is that transformation reaches back into the past and transforms it. In fact, if you are transformed, then you know that what you were doing all along the line was being transformed, and the way you know that is because you are transformed.

Since transformation is not an event, it can't HAPPEN—it can only BE. One can't BECOME transformed, one can only BE transformed. So, if one cannot become transformed and can only BE transformed, and if, in fact one is transformed, then one must have ALWAYS been transformed. It also follows that if one is NOT transformed, then one was NEVER transformed. The way I knew that what might have looked like transformation 13 years ago couldn't have been transformation is because it ended.

So what happened to me 13 years ago was a peak experience and pretty soon I had it symbolized and conceptualized well enough so that it went away. I'm very pleased that I had it. It was very, very valuable to me, and it gave me the impetus to go looking and to discover transformation as context rather than "transformation" as an event. I spent the next eight years looking for that experience again, and I never got it back.

What I did get five years ago was transformation—and what happened five years ago was that I EXPERIENCED transformation, not as an experience but as an abstraction. Experience, or life, comes from generating principles, or, as I like to call them, "abstractions." Only generating principles, abstractions, have the power to create or to generate experience—that is, to generate life. Concepts give you the ability to EXPLAIN life. Abstractions give you the power to CREATE life.

So, true transformation is the RECOVERY by the self of the principles with which the self creates itself. Transformation is the self as the self. Transformation is the shift FROM the identification of self as a thing, a position, an event or even a process—to just being. True transformation is the SPACE in which life occurs. THAT is what est is actually about. That is what the est training which you went through is about, if you are looking for an explanation of it.[6]

I readily acknowledge that for most of us this is heavy reading. However, personally, it is useful for me to relate what he is saying to what Jesus said was to be the experience of those who really got what the Savior was talking about.

Jesus testified that he and his Father were *one,* which is a way of saying, one self. When the crowds objected to such statements by trying to stone him to death, he declared, "Is it not written in your law, 'I said, Ye are gods?' If he called them gods unto whom the word of God came . . . say ye of him whom the Father hath sanctified and sent into the world, 'Thou blasphemest' because I said, I am the Son of God?'"[7] In this context, the Word of God is more than mere divine information. Jesus is, himself, called the Word. Could it be that the light of God, the true mystery of godliness, would be what Werner chooses to call "abstractions," generating principles out of which Life creates life, that of which Jesus Christ was the manifestation and demonstration. Jesus also calls it living water and the bread of life.

At the Last Supper Jesus instructed his untransformed disciples to experience themselves as individual branches of one vine. "I am the vine, ye are the branches. He that abideth (consciously experiences) in me and *I in him,* the same bringeth forth much fruit, for without me ye can do nothing. If a man abide not in me, he is cast forth as a (separate) branch and is withered."[8]

"Much fruit" is perfect agape, which we will consider in the next chapter.

1. Graduate Review, April 1977, page 6
2. John 14:7-11
3. John 17:21
4. John 14:6 & 20
5. I John 1:5-6
6. Graduate Review, November 1976, pp. 1 & 2
7. John 13:29-36
8. John 15:5-6

CHAPTER 7

Perfect Love Without Fear

In Werner's description of his peak experience in 1963 and his transformation in 1971, he did not mention the word "love" once, yet that is really all he was talking about. He was not talking about the kind of love most of us experience, but the kind of love that Jesus talked about. To understand this, let us take a look at the meaning of the word.

Unfortunately, English has only the word "love" to describe a very wide range of meanings. The old Greek language in which our New Testament manuscripts are written had four different words to describe four entirely different kinds of love. The first three are

Eros: physical attraction between the sexes

Storge: family affection, attachment

Philia: approval, cherish, adore

All of these are feelings that happen to us, like "falling in love." They all have to do with a feeling of warmth, attachment, enjoyment. Through them we obtain our greatest pleasures, feel our greatest needs and also experience our greatest emotional pains when the objects of these affections are taken away from us.

So when we are told to love God with all of our hearts and to love our neighbors as ourselves, we think we know what is expected of us. We are to have these warm feelings to God and to His creations, including those who despitefully use us. There are those times, when we are particularly inspired by an uplifting experience, that we seem able to attain such harmonious feelings to all creatures. Yet the feelings do not last, especially when we are in the midst of aggravating circumstances. Sometimes we can keep our cool, if not our affection, while other times we are really upset, angry and "mad as the devil."

These feelings and thoughts which go with eros, storge and philia are all rather mechanical functions of the mind and body. As pleasant as they may be, there is little real virtue in such love since each just happens. These three words were the most commonly used words for love in the Greek language. The ancient Greeks seldom used the fourth word which does not describe a feeling. It describes more of an attitude or point of view. One might say a very harmonious point of view. We have referred to that Greek word in previous chapters. It is AGAPE, usually pronounced as aw-gaw-pay'.

Agape has to do with understanding, light, compassion. It is a way of seeing rather than a way of feeling. To the natural man, agape is the ability to put oneself in other peoples' moccasins, to appreciate their point of view. It is to recognize that what people do, at the moment they are doing it, they see it as right, proper or at least justified. They may not see it that way a moment or a day later, but at the moment of doing, people do that which is "right," meaning the most justified, for the way the situation looks to them at that time, place and circumstances. That does not mean that they are right, that it is proper, or that it should be justified—from our point of view. It means that from their point of view it is.

Our greatest hate is reserved for those who we feel know what we know is right but go on doing wrong anyway. That is what really burns us up. In fact, if you really watch your upsets carefully, you will find that is what the anger is all about. We do not get angry when we fully realize the offending person actually does not know any better. We boil on the inside when we think someone really knows better and is doing it anyway. Although it may be true that he might have known "better" than he did, under the circumstances, everything considered, what he did was to him the most "right" thing to do. That may be a little hard for some of us to accept at first thought. However, if we check oursleves out, we will see that at the moment of doing anything we really feel that it is the best of two goods or the least of two evils.

When Jesus said to "love your enemies," he did not use the word philia, which would mean to approve and cherish our enemies. He said agape our enemies, which is to really understnad our enemies. When we do, it is very natural to bless them, do good to them and pray for them. Eros, storge and philia, without agape, lead to resentment, jealousy, competition, indulgence, conflict and other forms of emotional disturbance. However, when eros, storge and philia are accompanied with agape, then a relationship is one of a fuller acceptance and sharing rather than suspicion and exploitation.

This is the way agape-love works for "getting better" on the milk level. It is an essential first step to lighten our heavy load of judging good and evil. Most of us have enough accounts-receivable to fill many ledgers because of all the things others owe us for the wrongs we think they knowingly and unjustly inflicted upon us. Thus, Jesus included the plea in the Lord's prayer, "forgive us our debts as we forgive our debtors." Then he emphasized the eternal law of balance, "For if ye forgive men their trespasses, your heavenly Father will also forgive you, but if ye forgive not men their trespasses, neither will your Father forgive your trespasses."[1] On the milk level, that sounds like Jesus is saying that it is good to forgive for we will receive the Father's mercy and it is bad not to forgive for we will receive the Father's revenge. For those who know only the double mind of the Tree of Knowledge, it would be intended to sound just that way.

We have mentioned that the same words have totally different meanings when used on different levels of truth. Agape-love is one of the most significant examples of this. On the meat or hidden level of truth, agape-love means more than understanding that we are really all alike. It means understanding that we are really all the SAME SELF. We see in total unity, without division. This is why John could talk about PERFECT AGAPE and why perfect love casts out all fear. This is why I said that Werner was talking about love when he was talking about transformation.

In October of 1976, Werner traveled to the Far East to vist the two spiritual leaders of the Tibetan Buddhists, the Karmapa and the Dalai Lama. Previously he had visited the leaders of the Zen Buddhists in Japan. Werner has freely acknowledged his debt to oriental teachings in his own search for enlightenment. So in discussing some of his interesting observations of these visits, he brought up the subject of compassion, which is included in agape, and how it relates to transformation. Here is what he had to say:

> The principle of compassion is fundamental to the teachings of the Tibetan Buddhists. Part of what I've attempted to communicate about the Eastern disciplines is that we in the West have often misunderstood the Buddhist notion of compassion and have taken it to mean "sympathy" or a feeling-sorry-for, or a kind of need to humiliate ourselves, or something in that area.
>
> My experience, particularly with the Tibetan Buddhists but also with the Zen Buddhists, is that compassion is seen as a very positive state. In other words, one comes back from nirvana or enlightenment, or non-attchment to the world, TO the world not as a sacrifice and not as having sacrificed it all, but as being able to see what's appropriate to BEING, in terms of making a contribution to people, to society and to the world. It's not at all like a burden or something you have to give up. When you're able to see what's appropriate to being in the world, you then see that you are privileged to be able to DO something . . .
>
> They have a true sense of compassion, of wanting it to work for everyone. They were THRILLED about what we're doing here. Literally thrilled. There was not even a little twinge of jealousy, or "Yes, but that's not Buddhism," or any of that stuff . . .
>
> Compassion relates to what the self is. Self-realization is often misunderstood in the West to be something which happens in the location you think of as "yourself." Our thinking goes something like this: That thing over there is you, and this thing over here is me.
>
> In the experience of enlightenment, the self ceases to be a thing stuck in a particular location or position. You are no longer that thing over there and I this thing over here. Instead, I experience mySelf as the space which that thing I call "you" and that thing I call "me" exists. As that unfolds, you have less and less attachment to that position, that thing which you have called yourSelf. Finally, there's no real

distinction, in terms of what's important, between the thing you call yourSelf and the thing you call somebody else. That dichotomy begins to break down. When I discover MY self and when you discover YOUR self, you and I will discover the same self.

So then compassion becomes very NATURAL. Not something you do. In other words, one doesn't now act compassionate—one is compassionate as one's self. The self is compassionate, in that the self recognizes ALL as itself.

You don't wear a badge that says, "I am compassionate." You don't wear a badge that says, "I love others." It's really a very natural thing—and that's the way it was with the Tibetan Buddhists, really natural. I just loved that they could be excited about ANYTHING that could produce true enlightenment—whether it was in the East or in the West, or whatever it was.

I thought it was particularly beautiful that they could acknowledge est as something that works very rapidly, which has very little tradition of its own and almost no ritual—all of which is so very different from Tibetan Buddhism. They have a LONG tradition and a LOT of ritual. Their practice is arduous and certainly long. And there was just no problem. They weren't made wrong, they weren't offended, they didn't feel any competition with something that seemed to deliver value to people in a very rapid way with very little tradition and almost no ritual and not a lot of time. They just loved it. They thought it was great . . .

We in the West have this really strange notion that it's "good" to be compassionate; and therefore "bad" NOT to be compassionate. And the whole meaning of compassion is lost if you make it "good" or "bad," to put it in more accurate terms—if you make it righteous.

Being compassionate is in no way "right" or righteous. It is natural. Therefore, those who lack compassion should not be made wrong, should not be made bad, but should be understood to be lacking in naturalness. When whoever lacks compassion discovers his or her self, compassion will be experienced and expressed as a natural attribute of self.[2]

Agape, union, compassion, understanding—perfect love. As Jesus declared, "If therefore thine eye be single, thy whole body shall be full of light,"NATURALLY.

John, who was appropriately called John the Beloved, had the most explicit words on the hidden wisdom of perfect love. He declared that God is love. Love, true agape, is total union. God is Source, Creator, the ground of all being. "God is Agape; and he that dwelleth in agape dwelleth in God and God in him. Herein is our agape MADE PERFECT, that we may have boldness in the day of judgment; because AS HE IS, SO ARE WE IN THIS WORLD. There is NO FEAR IN AGAPE; but PERFECT AGAPE CASTETH OUT FEAR; because fear hath torment. He that feareth is not made perfect in agape."[3]

Where fear is natural, agape is not natural. One is of the natural man, one is of the spiritual man. One is the Tree of Knowledge of Good and Evil and one is of the Tree of Life.

---

1. Matt. 6:11-15
2. Graduate Review, April 1977, pp. 4, 5 & 7
3. I John 4:16-18

CHAPTER 8

The Illusion of Obedience

Agape is being at union or oneness with what is. When we are at odds with what is, we are trying to be in union or oneness with what is not. That is an appropriate definition for an illusion. The double mind is convinced that it is not filled with illusions because it has constantly sought for "the truth and nothing but the truth."

Jesus said, "Ye shall know the truth and the truth shall make you free." We interpret that to mean that if we prove what is truth, we can use the truth to get better and better until we are free. What we fail to understand is that the truth is what is. To know the truth is to truly and freely experience what is. In doing so, we are free. We may not be comfortable, ideal, rich or whatever. Neither are we burdened, struggling, resisting nor anxious.

In contrast to this, the double mind is constantly trying to FIND the truth, to conclusively conceptualize as to the good and bad, the truth and false of everything. The mind is so intoxicated with the need to be right that it is willing to do anything to prove that what it believes SHOULD be true IS true. Using logic, which starts with an assumption and ends with a conclusion, the mind can PROVE anything—absolutely anything—to be the truth. It is the blind leading the blind and both fall in the ditch. When one experiences the notion that the self is one with all truth, therefore "knows" all truth, then the only task at hand is to discover the barriers to "knowing" what we know. These barriers are called illusions, misconceptions.

The higher, hidden wisdom, the teaching of enlightenment, deals almost exclusively with the barriers, the misconceptions and illusions. Awakening from the dead is a process of discovering WHAT IS NOT THE TRUTH. That is something even the conditioned mind CAN DO. For example, most of us once lived in a world where we "knew" there was a Santa Claus. One day we discovered that such a belief was an illusion. We saw what was not the truth and THAT was the TRUTH. Afterwards, our world was a different world, a little closer to the real world. Transformation "is" when the illusions about self become transparent, which removes them completely. It is just being who and what we already are. We do not become who we are by finding out who we are. As they say in est, the process has more to do with finding out who and what we ARE NOT.

For many seekers, enlightenment is supposed to be something acquired and developed within us. In the wisdom teachings, it is compared to a priceless treasure hidden in the ground. The process is to remove the barrier by getting the dirt and rocks out of the way. The treasure is not *constructed,* it is *revealed* by being uncovered. It is also compared to a pearl of great price which, when found, a person sells ALL of his other pearls for the price to obtain the one. The other pearls are all our rich treasures, called beliefs, which are exchanged for the single truth.

Illusions and misconceptions are not bad, just as the other pearls or the dirt and rocks are not bad. They are merely the barriers, the obstacles which exist in this game called life. Without obstacles there is no game. We win a game by getting through and around the obstacles. There is no winning if there can be no losing and the barriers can keep us from winning. So we can see through another illusion—that illusions are bad. So now then we can believe that illusions are good. That would be another illusion. Illusions just are.

In contrast to the usual search for truth—which is an endless and laborious search—the search for illusions can be one round of fun. We find that we have been playing one joke after another on ourselves. Sometimes the jokes get a little cruel, yet we still get to have the last laugh. All that is necessary to find an illusion is to find a belief.

An example of a very tenacious belief is the idea "I've got to!" Implied and expressed in a vast majority of our thoughts is the illusion that we have *got to* do anything. We do not even "got to" live. We can check out anytime we choose and we may check out even though we do not choose. So it is inaccurate to say we have got to live. When we are visiting a friend and want to leave, we say, "I'm sorry, but I've really GOT TO GO." That is a lie. We say it to escape the responsibility for WANTING TO GO. We want it to appear that we would stay if we could do what we wanted BUT we can't do what we want. The truth is that we never, ever do anything except what we WANT TO DO—MOST OF ALL. To think otherwise is another of our illusions. We think we are hardly ever able to do what we really want. What we really mean is that we do not usually like what we really want. So for example, we go to the job to earn our livelihood even though we might have more fun at the beach. We go to the job instead of the beach because we want to, we choose to, and not because we have "got to." People wait most of their lives to BE FREE so they can do what they "want." The joke is that they have been doing only what they want all their lives. One of the most difficult ideas to accept is that we are already free.

The path of discovery is fascinating since we find beliefs by the hundreds that we never realized were beliefs. Each time we discover the truth of what is NOT TRUE, we experience an expansion of the space in which the events of our life occur. This is the process of liberation. The truth makes us free.

I used to think that our greatest requirement and spiritual achievement was obedience to the will of God, meaning primarily keeping the commandments. Trying to do so certainly has value as a beginning school and for getting better, as well as finding order in one's life. We are convinced that obedience to God is the ultimate virtue and integrity. This is another of our great illusions.

In obedience, one is at the effect of an order. There is no integrity in being at effect. True integrity exists only when one is responsible as the initiator, the source. To obey is to copy or follow the initiation of another. That does not make obedience wrong or bad. It just is not integrity. Most of us have failed to realize that one can follow the rules—without being obedient.

For example, if a person does not rob a bank only because it is against the law, he is a bank robber at heart who is afraid to rob a bank because of the threat of the law. Since most of us do not rob banks for the simple reason that it is not our money, our lack of bank robbing is NOT OBEDIENCE TO THE LAW. It is the integrity of our own responsibility. We just choose to leave other people's money alone. We are the source of our choice.

What happened in Nazi Germany before and during World War II was a violent demonstration of the absence of integrity in obedience. In the war-criminal trials after the war, the German leaders excused themselves by saying that they were just being obedient to orders. Whose orders? Their god, the Fuehrer. The Mafia is another demonstration of obedience without integrity. "Nothing personal," the hit man says, "just following orders."

Actually, if it were obedience God was after, that would be the easiest and simplest quality to achieve. A hypnotist proves how completely we can be made obedient and love it. Yet in the hypnotic demonstration, there is the total absence of integrity. Then one might ask, "But God wants us to use our free will to obey." The truth is that the very structure of obedience is to deny free will. The relationship implies master and servant, reward and punishment. When a bandit puts a gun in your ribs and demands your money, you either obey and receive the reward of keeping your life or disobey and pay with your life. As long as we OBEY God, are we really in a different relationship? We are at the effect of His demands, wanting His rewards and fearing His penalties.

If you object to that notion, then ask yourself if it is possible to "obey" the command to love, to be patient, to have faith and trust? Love, patience, faith and trust are qualities of being rather than obedience by doing. Someone might quote the statement by Paul about Jesus, that "though he were a Son, yet learned he obedience by the things which he suffered."[1] The Greek word peitho which is translated here as obedience is almost always translated as to "be persuaded or convinced to trust", "to have confidence." Jesus grew in confidence and trust of Life, the Father, by difficult experiences. That is what Paul seems to really be saying. Paul frequently stressed that we are not to be slaves but joint-heirs, meaning equal to Christ, to be responsible as co-owners.

Then why does God give all of these commandments? Could it be that we are such believers in the illusion of absolute good and evil that we have wanted it no other way. We have claimed that if God will just tell us what is *good,* we will certainly do the good and if He tells us what is *bad* we will certainly not do the bad. We completely forget that even after we were forbidden to partake of the knowledge of good and evil, we expect God to give us that knowledge.

So do you really see what has taken place? We have obtained divine orders all right. The most extreme example of this is when the Israelites were led by Moses out of Egypt. They couldn't even be satisfied with ten, so they kept asking until they got about ten thousand, literally. It takes twenty-seven chapters of Leviticus to lay them out. Then their wise men went to work and split them up into ten times that number.

Most of us have heard the story about the man coming out of church after the preacher had given a hell-fire sermon on keeping the Ten Commandments. He mumbled to his wife, "Well, anyway, I haven't made any graven images!" Do you want to bet? No one who thinks he is his mind and body can "have no other gods before me," "keep the sabbath day

HOLY," "HONOR thy father and thy mother,"
"not kill," "not commit adultery" (particularly as
Jesus defined it), "not steal," "not bear false witness" (called gossip), nor "covet thy neighbor's good
fortune" (called envy). In another chapter, we will
deal with the little item of "taking the name of God in
vain" because we blow that one even without profan-
ity.

So what is to be done? Obviously the Ten Commandments make a great deal of sense. They are very
excellent ideas which can give order and stability to
our lives and to a society. However, the Ten Commandments, as rigid statements of good and evil, the
violation of which is supposed to make us evil and the
keeping of which will make us good, are unworkable.
Only when we understand and accept these ideas as
our own, personal AGREEMENTS, can they have
life and meaning, love and nourishment. Then these
ideas become our OWN intentions. Keeping an
agreement is not seen as right versus wrong. It is seen
as being responsible, being the chooser of our intentions.

When people start the est training, they are authoritatively read a whole list of agreements. The
sternness of the training supervisor, the soberness of
the training assistants and the formality of the seating
seem to imply that the items are arbitrary orders that
everyone must obey. (Later the trainer will crypti-
cally remind everyone that what they are doing in the
training is not necessarily WHAT they are doing.) To
many of the trainees, the est "commandments" are
unfair, unnecessary, unreasonable and probably un-
American. Some want the rules clarified, others want
them modified, still others want them nullified. Why

can't we sit by a friend? Why can't I have a watch in here? Why can't I meditate during the week? The simple answer is that the agreements are what they are because they WORK. The trainees are asked not to accept these as the rules of est but to accept them as their own agreements or intentions for the duration of the training. "If you want the training to work, keep the agreements."

Later in the training a majority will stand to confess that they broke this or the other agreement. The trainer acknowledges the reports and merely reminds everyone that it is their responsiblity to choose these agreements as their own. est does not care what they do with them. The agreements provide the trainees with the opportunity to get in touch with what is between them and keeping agreements. Those who do not break their agreements are reminded that they may be just as stuck in keeping agreements—being obedient—as the others are in breaking their agreements—being disobedient.

The whole process on agreements was very valuable to me. I got in touch with the fact that I had the idea that an agreement is a contractual guarantee. When I have broken an agreement, I have broken my word and that is not good at all. I began to see that such was another one of my beliefs of the double mind. In reality, an agreement is a communication about what we choose as our intention in the future. No one can absolutely guarantee anything in the future. To do so is an illusion. We may not even be alive, for one thing. Breaking agreements, being inevitable, is neither good nor bad. What is necessary for relationships to work is that the individuals be responsible for their agreements. Being responsible means that we recognize that we choose the agreement. We are the source. We are not responsible when we make others the source by saying, "I did not want to do it but he made me agree to do it." No one can MAKE us agree. We CHOOSE.

So being responsible for our very own agreements, if we find that we have broken one, we can choose to act responsibly about it. This means to do whatever is necessary to take care of the situation resulting from the broken agreement. Our lives do not work, not just because we do not keep agreements, but also because we do not clean them up when they are broken. For example, if I have failed to keep an appointment, I can try to ignore it, claim the other person misunderstood or lie about what distracted me, anything to escape being made wrong. Or I can accept total responsibility (which has nothing to do with blame) for the broken agreement, show appropriate consideration for the other person's inconvenience and do whatever can be done to go on from there.

When individuals look to God to spell out the strict rules of what is good and evil so that they can be good by obeying and not be bad by disobeying, they have accepted a trap of "death," a separator from aliveness. Life is never rigid. What may be appropriate one time could be very harmful another time. For example, should I never kill, regardless of the circumstances? Should I always honor my father and mother, no matter what? Should I always tell the truth about others? Should I never want what others have? I am not giving these questions to justify breaking any of the laws—Lord knows we do that enough anyway. My point is that every law demonstrates that a rigid, absolute, never alterable rule of what is right and good is an illusion. There is NO SUCH KNOWLEDGE.

In case you want to check it out, the only commandment against which there is no exception, no excess, no possible contradiction is AGAPE—perfect love. We can even have too much of the other kinds of love—eros, storge or philia—those which have to do with emotion and desire, but never too much UNDERSTANDING. That is why the Tree of Life can really be called the Tree of Love (code name: Aliveness) and why the Tree of Knowledge of Good and Evil can be called the Tree of Obedience (code name: Illusion).

The difference between these two ways of accepting the commandments is truly the difference between living and dying, being complete and being incomplete. By the Tree of Life we get away from judging, needing to be right and continually comparing what "is" with what "ought to be."

Now we are ready to discuss what may be the major purpose for divine "commandments." We have acknowledged that the outer purpose of the commandments is to serve as a valuable basis for self-discipline and order in a society of greedy, self-seeking people. However, if a person is really honest and awake, he will soon recognize that no one can and no one does obey them all. Yet the law specifically allows no margin for error. "Be ye therefore perfect!" God cannot "look upon sin with the least degree of allowance!" To those who insist that the law must be the law—no exceptions, no excuses, no rationalizations—James asks them to remember that "whosoever shall keep the whole law, and yet offend in one point, HE IS GUILTY OF ALL."[2] The total impossibility of keeping all of the law reveals that there is no perfection through it, the defined knowledge of good and evil.

Paul, who had been a perfectionist in the law of obedience until his liberation, discovered this hidden purpose of the law. He said, "Now we know that what things soever the law saith, it saith to them who are under the law, that EVERY MOUTH may be stopped and ALL the world may become GUILTY before God. Therefore by the deeds (obedience) of the law there shall no flesh be justified in his sight, for by the law IS THE KNOWLEDGE OF SIN."[3]

Do you have an idea of what "knowledge of sin" means? "Everyone knows" that sin means doing bad things or not doing good things. Sin to most people means doing wrong. The Greek word being translated is hamartia which means missing the mark. We might say it in modern terminology, MISSING THE POINT. When we turned from the Tree of Life to the Tree of Knowledge we really missed the whole point of living. That is our ORIGINAL SIN. In the words of Werner, we gave up aliveness for being right. So Paul is telling us that the law of commandments was given to us to allow us to discover once and for all that obedience does not work. In this way we may gain the knowledge of sin, knowing how we missed the point.

Few people make such a discovery since they are not really honest about their "guilt." They are lulled into a false security by their lying to themselves that they are obedient enough. The Jewish people were in such a state when Jesus started his ministry. Since Jesus was teaching the multitudes the outer truth, he took them even higher on the law of obedience. He told them that he had not come to destroy the law. He had come to fulfill it. (Incidentally, it is a notion of est that when something is fulfilled and completed, it disappears.) So what did Jesus do? He not only supported and acknowledged the law, he increased its demands. He went beyond what we *do* to include what are our *intentions*. The major portion of this instruction is included in the Sermon on the Mount, found in Matthew, chapters five to seven. It includes such famous sections as the Beatitudes, the Lord's Prayer, "Be ye therefore perfect," The Golden Rule, and ends with the warning that those foolish people who do not do these things would be like the man who built his house on the sand and was destroyed by the storm.

I was once talking to a good friend of mine who was a youth leader in another denomination. I had been sharing with him my ideas about the degree of spirituality Christ said is necessary to make the Gospel work. After some discussion, he said, "I hear what you are saying, Max, but you are way over my head. My religion is just the simple words of Jesus that he gave in the Sermon on the Mount. I figure that by just doing what he says there I am being true to my Lord."

Since I was very familiar with those three chapters, I asked him if he would like to read them over with me. As we did so, he acknowledged that he had totally underestimated the difficulty such instructions would involve. Following is a line by line listing of Christ's new "standards" in the Sermon on the Mount.

1. Blessed are the *poor in spirit*, those that *mourn*, the *meek*, those who *hunger* and *thirst* after righteousness, the

merciful, the *pure* in heart, the *peacemakers* and they who are persecuted for righteousness sake.

2. Let your light so shine before men that they may see your good works and glorify your Father which is in heaven.

3. Think not that I am come to destroy the law. I am come to fulfill. Whosoever, therefore shall *break one of these least commandments* and shall teach men so, he shall be called least in the kingdom of heaven.

4. Whosoever is *angry* with his brother without a cause shall be in danger of the judgment.

5. Whosoever shall say, thou *fool,* shall be in danger of hell fire.

6. *Agree* with thine adversary quickly.

7. Whosoever *looketh* on a woman to lust after her hath committed adultery with her already in his heart.

8. If thy right eye offend thee, *pluck it out* and cast it from thee.

9. If they right hand offend thee, *cut it off* and cast it from thee.

10. Whosoever shall *put away* his wife, saving for the cause of fornication, causeth her to commit adultery and whoever shall marry her that is divorced committeth adultery.

11. *Swear* (an oath) *not at all,* neither by heaven, nor by the earth, by Jerusalem, nor by thy head, but let your communications be yea (for) yea; nay (for) nay, for whatsoever is more than these cometh of evil.

12. *Resist not evil* but whosoever shall smite thee on thy right cheek, turn to him the other also.

13. If any man sue thee at the law and take away thy coat, *let him have* thy cloak also.

14. Whosoever shall compel thee to go a mile, *go* with him twain.

15. *Give* to him that asketh thee and from him that would borrow of thee turn not thou away.

16. *Love* your enemies, *bless* them that curse you, *do good* to them that hate you and *pray* for them which despitefully use you and persecute you.

17. *Be ye* therefore *perfect,* even as your Father which is in heaven is perfect.

18. *Do not* your alms before men to be seen of them. When

thou doest alms *let not* thy left hand know what thy right hand doeth.

19. When thou prayest, enter into thy closet, *use not* vain repetitions.

20. *Forgive* men their trespasses.

21. When thou fast, *appear not* unto men to fast, but anoint thine head and wash thy face.

22. *Lay not up* for yourselves treasures upon earth but *lay up* treasures in heaven.

23. If thy eye be *single,* thy whole body shall be full of light. No man can serve God and mammon.

24. Take *no thought* for your life, what ye shall eat or what ye shall drink nor yet for your body. Take *no thought* saying, "What shall we eat? What shall we drink? or Wherewithal shall we be clothed? but *seek ye first* the kingdom of God and his righteousness and all these things shall be added unto you.

25. Take therefore *no thought* for the morrow.

26. *Judge not* that ye be not judged. First *cast out* the beam out of thine own eye and then thou shalt see clearly to cast out the mote out of thy brother's eye.

27. *Give not* that which is holy unto the dogs neither cast ye pearls before swine.

28. *Ask* and it shall be given you, *seek* and ye shall find, *knock* and it shall be opened unto you.

29. *All things* whatsoever ye would that men should do to you, do ye even so to them.

30. *Enter ye in* at the strait gate for wide is the gate and broad is the way that leadeth to destruction.

When we read these authoritative orders carefully and honestly, we might exclaim with the disciples when Jesus remarked that it would be easier for a camel to go through the eye of a needle than for a rich man (who has many pearls of belief about good and evil) to enter into the kingdom of God. They asked, WHO THEN CAN BE SAVED?[4]

What would Jesus' answer be to such a complaint? Simply this—"With MEN THIS IS IMPOSSIBLE,

but with GOD ALL THINGS ARE POSSIBLE."[5]
So there is a way! Paul said it is by GRACE
THROUGH FAITH. As a matter of fact, there is no
other way. Yet the double mind which may finally see
the futility of trying to be saved by the illusion of
obedience, tries to be saved by his interpretation of
what is meant by "grace through faith." So the mind
comes up with another belief which is another
illusion—missing the point. We might call it the illusion of faith and we will deal with it in the next
chapter.

Later we will also take the Sermon on the Mount
and show how meaningful these instructions are for
those who see them as words of life rather than
knowledge of good and evil.

---

1. Hebrews 5:8
2. James 2:1
3. Romans 3:19-20
4. Matt. 19:25
5. Matt. 19:26

CHAPTER 9
The Illusion of Faith

If there is anything most Christians are depending upon to get them through the Judgment Day it is their faith. In fact many churches have joyfully proclaimed the inability of obedience—called works—to save anyone, stressing that we are saved by grace through faith. One of the most memorized scriptures is "for God so loved the world, that he gave his only begotton Son, that whosoever BELIEVETH in him should not perish but have everlasting life."[1]

Paul, who wrote about half of the New Testament, appreciated this aspect of the Good News so well that he referred to it often in such words as: "For by grace are ye saved through faith and that not of yourselves, it is a gift of God; not of works lest any man should boast."[2]

Though many quote this verse, few are familiar with Paul's next point when he adds, "For we are his workmanship, created in Christ Jesus UNTO GOOD WORKS, which God hath before ordained that we should walk in them."[3]

James saw how the double mind greatly distorts the teachings about the regenerative power of "belief," and he wrote very frankly about it. Not many modern believers care much for the little book of James because he challenges their illusions. "What doth it profit, my brethren, though a man say he hath faith and have not works? Can faith save him? . . . Show me thy faith without thy works and I will show thee my faith by my works. Thou believest that there is

one God, thou doest well. The devils also believe and
TREMBLE."[4]

. Paul was saying no less. He prayed that "Jesus . . .
(would) make you PERFECT IN EVERY GOOD
WORK to do his will, working in you that which is
well pleasing in his sight."[5] There we have that word
"perfect" again.

Actually, the difficulty in understanding what is
really involved in transformation and rebirth is increased by the extensive use of the English word
"belief" in our translations. Belief, as defined in our
dictionary, is "the acceptance of an alleged fact or
body of facts as true without positive knowledge or
proof." Faith is "the confidence and assurance we
have in our beliefs." That may well be what people
have, but that does not seem to accurately describe
the characteristic or quality which makes everlasting
life a reality.

Paul declared that "faith" is much more than acceptance, it is the very substance and evidence, in
and of itself. Even more emphatic, Jesus specifically
described the effect such true "belief" produces in a
person's life, right here and now. We might call it a
"test" for the presence of faith. Jesus said in all
seriousness at the Last Supper, "Verily, verily (truly,
truly), I say unto you, he that BELIEVETH ON
ME, the WORKS that I do SHALL HE DO ALSO:
and GREATER works than these shall he do, because I go unto my Father."[6]

In other words, if I understand him correctly, if we
don't do the works that Jesus did, let alone greater
works, then we have clear evidence that we are
lacking in this quality he called "believeth on me."
So what were the works of Jesus? He described them

as his witness to the world. "The blind receive their sight and the lame walk, the lepers are cleansed and the deaf hear, the dead are raised up and the poor have the gospel preached to them."[7]

After Christ's resurrection, he commissioned his disciples to go to all the world "and preach the gospel to every creature. He that believeth and is baptized shall be saved but he that believeth not shall be DAMNED. And these signs shall follow *them that BELIEVE;* in my name shall they cast out devils; they shall speak with new tongues; they shall take up serpents and if they drink any deadly thing, it shall not hurt them; they shall lay hands on the sick and they shall recover."[8]

I once heard about a beautiful gothic church in New York that had those words engraved on its corner stone. A reporter happened by and was impressed. He knocked at the rectory and inquired, "Is it true?" When the pastor seemed bewildered, the reporter responded, "I was just curious whether it really worked like that or whether it was false advertising."

The minister is not the only one who would be surprised by such a question. Those assurances of miraculous activity sound unattainable or incomprehensible to most modern followers of the Galilean carpenter. Surely, we exclaim, such a test for belief is not fulfillable for the ordinary person! True! The ordinary person is a natural, carnal man. Jesus was talking about something that transformed people into spiritual beings who would accomplish spiritual activity as easily and naturally as he did.

We so easily forget that there were great numbers during that first generation who demonstrated the accuracy of this prophetic declaration. You can read some of the accounts for yourself in the Acts of the Apostles. Here are a few:

> And by the hands of the apostles were many signs and wonders wrought among the people . . . insomuch that they brought forth the sick into the streets and laid them on beds and couches, that at the least the shadow of Peter passing by might overshadow some of them. There came also a multitude out of the cities round about unto Jerusalem, bringing sick folks and them which were vexed with unclean spirits and they WERE HEALED EVERY ONE.[9]
>
> Steven, who was not one of the apostles, was "full of faith and power, did great wonders and miracles among the people."[10]
>
> Phillip, also not of the twelve, went to preach in Samaria. The people listened to his message, "seeing the miracles which he did, for unclean spirits, crying with loud voices, came out of many that were possessed with them, and many taken with palsy and that were lame were healed and there was GREAT JOY IN THE CITY."[11]

This is what happens, according to Jesus, when people really "believe," really have "faith." The record is clear for all to read and there is much, much more. Yet so few have bothered to match their belief with the test. If they did, they might possibly check to see if their "faith" is only another of their valued illusions.

Please remember, I am not trying to convince anyone that they need more, better or different faith. I have a notion, like Werner talks about our already knowing the truth, that we also have all the real "faith" there is. Our situation is that we have barriers to experiencing that faith. We do not need to create more or better "faith," just get the illusions out of the way which prevent us from getting in touch with it.

As many are aware, there are some remarkable people around today who are experiencing healings, tongues, prophesying, and other spiritual blessings. Most Christians keep their distance. They are turned off by some of the carnival, hoop-te-da that often goes with the enthusiastic build up. Others seriously doubt the validity of the miraculous claims, yet I personally have seen very convincing evidence. So is this the level of miraculous activity I am talking about?

No, not in most cases at least. I am very familiar with many of these movements and individuals. The work being done is really amazing. Lives are truly made more meaningful and hope is regained. I enjoy being around them and truly support their activity. I mean nothing disparaging when I suggest that most of them are still functioning on only the second level of truth. This is what Christ's own disciples were doing for the three eventful years they were his close friends and students, so that is not too shabby!

Signs and wonders are very heady things. Those people who have not left the first level of truth, the obedience level, are usually disturbed or threatened by those who do miracles. They prefer the law of obedience because it is something they can put together and control like nuts and bolts (called jots and tittles). To them, miracles and revelations are too unpredictable and uncontrollable. The people who move to the second level of truth have just the opposite reaction to the marvelous demonstrations of "divine intervention." They are convinced that it is the outside power of God that comes into them to heal, reveal, redeem and glorify. So they react with great emotional ecstasy, truly thrilled by the success of their faith.

Such, we are told, was the great joy felt by the twelve disciples during those three years when they were sent out by Jesus with power and authority "to heal the sick, cleanse the the lepers, raise the dead, cast out devils. Freely ye have received. freely give."[12] "And they departed and went through the towns, preaching the gospel and healing EVERY WHERE."[13] Jesus added to their number seventy more disciples, telling them to go into any house that would receive them "and heal the sick that are therein, and say unto them, the kingdom of God is come nigh unto you . . . And the seventy returned again with joy, saying, Lord, even the devils are subject unto us through thy name."[14]

I have repeated this story again to remind us that even after this, these same men were asking which one of them would be the greatest in the kingdom of heaven. Jesus rebuked them by taking a little youngster into their midst and then saying, "Verily I say unto you, EXCEPT YE BE CONVERTED AND BECOME AS LITTLE CHILDREN, ye shall not enter into the kingdom of heaven."[15] Even though they were doing miracles, they were yet to be converted.

At the Last Supper, Jesus said to Peter, the rock, "Simon, Simon, behold Satan hath desired to have you, that he may sift you as wheat. But I have prayed for thee, that thy faith fail not, and WHEN YOU ARE CONVERTED, strengthen thy bretheren."[16] It was also at that time, you will recall, when he told them that in their present state of being they could not yet bear the greater things he would be teaching them.

Not every attempt of the disciples to heal during this period was successful. One time when nine of them tried to cast out a "dumb spirit" from a raving boy, the boy got worse. The crowd reacted and began to get out of hand when Jesus came by and took command. He healed the boy and went with the disciples to a house. As soon as the group was inside, they asked, "Why could not we cast him out?" Jesus replied, "This kind can come forth by nothing but by prayer and fasting."[17]

I have an interesting notion about what happened. Jesus healed NATURALLY. For the disciples to heal, they required authority, meaning permission. If that did not work, they needed fasting and prayer. In our present day healing services, speaking in tongues and other spiritual gifts are not forthcoming unless the people are brought to a high state of anticipation. As we have previously discussed, the mind can create the experience to support its beliefs in what should happen. A "spirit of power" meeting is an orchestration set by the speakers, music, atmosphere and audience participation. The "revival" atmosphere is literally "spell-binding."

Psychologists are familiar with various stages of altered consciousness. As was demonstated with Kreskin, the natural man is very suggestive. One does not have to be hysterical to be "overcome". Under hypnosis, people have experienced marvelous physical and mental cures, extra-sensory preception, visions, a sense of spiritual rebirth, unknown languages, as well as many other presumed spiritual miracles. I have mentioned that the hypnotist functions by temporarily shutting off the "Not Go" part of the double mind to some degree, thus making the person a total believer. When the mind is single, even artificially so, it has partial access to infinite being, the true Self.

People can find many ways to get in a trance state. Meditation is now very popular. Church music is often spellbinding. Good preachers can be hypnotic. Going without sleep or food for a long period will "flip" one out, opening all kinds of doors. When one has gained an understanding of how the trance state is induced, it is incredibly fascinating to watch sincere professionals condition an audience. Of course, since these things are done for the glory of Christ, it is all justified as a way of getting the soul filled with the "Spirit of God." When the people are able to experience the miraculous, they "know" that Jesus truly lives within their hearts. They fail to realize that most other world religions, ancient or modern, have found ways to do the same things. This is why the religions, great and small, have commanded such total loyalty. Each group is convinced that such "out-of-the-world" experiences are unique to their faith and proof of their beliefs.

Again, I want to stress that these approaches to deeper experiences and miraculous powers are not bad in any way. They can be very marvelous. People's lives can be uplifted. Health and attitude can be enhanced. However, there are dangers to the use of the trance state if it is carelessly handled. This does happen sometimes. People may get over-zealous in taking others "up" without realizing that the individuals should also be carefully brought back down. The old black preachers of the South were true masters at this. They knew how to take their people up to a glorious state of frenzy, let them experience cosmic confidence and ecstasy, then gradually bring them back down to this muddy, double minded earth. If that is not done, it is possible for people to go out of a "peak experience" meeting and get back their double minds in such a way that they crash.

Even before I took the est training, I was aware that Werner also uses the advantages of an altered state of consciousness. It was not the "revival" kind used to induce a peak experience. It is strictly low key, designed to allow the barriers of the double mind to become more pliable. This is partially achieved by the formal pronouncement of the agreements, then using directed processes as well as the long physical and mental endurance.

Some critics have claimed that est is brainwashing through hypnotism. Although Werner does not argue with critics, a group of ten highly regarded members of the psychological and medical professions who had taken the training testified that it was their experience that est is just the opposite of brainwashing. They said that if it can be called anything, it should be called DE-HYPNOSIS. That was my own experience also.

The difference between est and a religious revival-type meeting is that est is designed to enable the individual to move beyond one's demanding NEEDS. Needs are what one knows would be good or bad in the future. Religious services are designed to help one fulfill one's NEEDS, getting the "good" and losing the "evil." Fasting, praying, praising, chanting, humming, dancing, singing and even a little drinking can sometimes produce the required "spiritual" state.

Certain drugs can do the same. "Getting it" in religion is usually getting WITH IT. "Getting it" in est is
getting OFF IT.

When Jesus gave his special students permission to
heal as he was doing, he enabled them to make up
their double minds. If that did not work in a given
case, they could finish the job with fasting and praying. It works. I have done it myself. The example I
gave of my daughter being instantly healed of polyps
was an example. I have experienced hundred of
others. I have also seen it fail to work more times
than not. I have seen amazing prophetic predictions
and visions come to pass and I have seen them completely miss. The miraculous level of truth does not
work consistently. If so, we would probably never
realize that the greater truth is yet to come.

Christ taught that when much is given, much is
required. Those who move up from the first level of
obedience to the second level of power by faith have
received much. If they do not move on to the next
level by being turned around, converted (as did the
disciples after the resurrection), they will gradually
lose what they had. When that happens, the "getting
filled" becomes more difficult and the miracles become less frequent. The person becomes fearful and
tries harder and harder, but in the wrong direction.
There is a temptation to cover-up the deficiency, first
by retelling the past glories, then "gilding the lily" a
bit, then finally some occasional trickery or staging.
Exaggeration appears justified, of course, since it is
good to build people's faith. Finally, most of it becomes fakery, even though they remain sincere.

This is where the profession of magicians originally
came from. Anciently, spiritual men demonstrated

complete power over reality, including death. Jesus was such a demonstration. The wise men from the East who visited the baby in Bethlehem were evidently of this caliber. They were called the MAGI, doers of the miraculous, true magicians. A commercial magician is one who openly pretends that he is a Magi and makes no claim to really being one. But merchants of faith claim to be real.

It is to this point that Jesus included in his Sermon on the Mount the warning, "Not every one that saith unto me, Lord, Lord, shall enter into the kingdom of heaven, but he that doeth the will of my Father which is in heaven. Many will say to me in that day, Lord, Lord, have we not prophesied in thy name and in thy name have cast out devils? And in thy name done many wonderful works? And then will I profess unto them, I NEVER KNEW YOU. Depart from me, ye that work iniquity."[18]

I think people have the illusion that faith is some magical mental magnet which attracts the blessings of heaven. People have a real ego trip when they believe that God cannot be happy unless they do the right things to please Him, and then He is supposed to be so delighted He will give them all kinds of pretty presents. This is the Santa Claus god of many—another illusion. Again, illusions are not bad. They can be very useful at certain stages of liberation.

Paul, who taught the milk but referred often to the meat, recognized that total union, agape, was the real characteristic of the full, spiritual man. He declared that belief and faith were to evaporate in the transforming experience of agape—which comes from knowing who we are. In his famous chapter in First Corinthians on agape, he describes the movement to this higher level of experience. In English, each agape is translated as the old English word, charity, which used to mean the same quality Werner described as the "compassion" of the Buddhists. "Though I speak with the tongues of men and of angels and have not agape (perfect love), I am become as sounding brass or a tinkling cymbal. And though I have the gift of prophecy and understand all mysteries and all knowledge and though I have all faith, so that I could remove mountains, and have not agape, I AM NOTHING. And though I bestow all my goods to feed the poor and though I give my body to be burned and have not agape it profiteth me NOTHING . . .

"Agape NEVER FAILETH. But whether there be prophecies, they shall fail, whether there be tongues, they shall cease; whether there be knowledge (of good and evil), it shall vanish away. For we know in part and we prophecy in part. But when that which is PERFECT (Agape) IS COME, that which is in part shall be done away. When I was a child, I spake as a child, I understood as a child, I thought as a child, but when I became a man (the true self), I put away childish things.

"For now we see through a glass, darkly, but THEN, FACE TO FACE. Now I know in part, but THEN SHALL I KNOW EVEN AS ALSO I AM KNOWN. Now abideth faith, hope and agape, these three, BUT THE GREATEST OF THESE IS AGAPE."[19]

We have mentioned that people on the obedience level are disturbed by the gifts of the Spirit. Those on the miraculous level are thrilled and fortified by divine manifestations. Those on the third or understanding level merely find it all very interesting. The fourth or transformed level find it all just very NATURAL. That is the way Jesus walked naturally on the water, fed the five thousand and raised the dead. This seems to have been the way that the Christ-men of the early church lived with the power of BEING.

1. John 3:16
2. Eph. 2:8-9
3. Eph. 2:10
4. James 2:14-19
5. Hebrews 13:20-21
6. John 14:12
7. Matt. 11:5
8. Mark 16:15-18
9. Acts 5:12-16
10. Acts 6:8
11. Acts 8:5-8
12. Matt. 10:8
13. Luke 9:1-6
14. Luke 10:8-17
15. Matt. 18:1-3
16. Luke 22:31
17. Mark 10:28-29
18. Matt. 7:21-23
19. I Cor. 13:1-13

CHAPTER 10

The Meaning of Christ

The third level of truth is understanding the hidden meaning of Christ. As we have mentioned, each level uses the same words with different meanings, each level dealing with "knowing the truth." Deeper truths do not contradict as much as they expand and enlarge. However, in the enlarged understanding comes something so much more significant and cosmic that the ideas of the prior level seem to pale to insignificance.

The literal level of obedience sees Christ as the son of the divine Monarch who has been sent down to pay the debt created by our sins and to provide the rules necessary to join him in re-entering the gates of the glorious kingdom of God. Christ is the leader, the example, the willing martyr and the hero. To take upon ourselves the name of Christ means to swear allegiance to his cause. Any sacrifice on our part should be made for such a savior. Most Christians in the last two thousand years have never known any other meaning for Jesus Christ.

The second level, the "spiritual" level of power by faith, sees the meaning of Christ in a more mystical way. Instead of Christ being only our leader and mediator before God, he is also our indwelling companion through his infinite presence, the Spirit of Truth, the Holy Ghost. Christ stands at the door of our hearts and knocks. If we will open the door, he will literally take up his abode within us, thereby enabling us to do his will and his work. In this way, his faith is our faith, as is also his wisdom, mercy, love and power. His "inner abiding" is demonstrated by numerous evidences, such as the burning in the bosom, fire or energy charging through the bones, ecstasy in the heart and confidence and assurance in the mind. To the gifted, his presence is known through the gifts of the Spirit, such as healing, tongues, prophesying, spiritual teaching, revelations and other miraculous experiences. The meaning of Jesus on this second level is that he is living in the world today by the indwelling of his spirit in the bodies of the faithful who make up his spiritual church, known as the mystical body of Christ. To take upon ourselves the name of Jesus Christ is to act AS HE, using his authority to call forth the will and blessings of heaven.

As we now come to the third level, let us remember that whatever it is, it was not taught directly until after the resurrection, when according to the writer of Acts, Jesus spent forty days with the disciples.[1] After Christ's ascension, the group of about one hundred and twenty waited for the anointing of light which occurred ten days later on the Jewish holy day of Pentecost.

It would be presumptuous of me to say that we will now discuss the hidden teachings which no one openly recorded. It does appear that John included some of the material in his writings, since he is acknowledged to have written on the deepest levels. Remember, the hidden teachings, which Paul called the meat, were discussed only privately among those who were perfect. Then how is one to know the hidden teachings?

There is an old saying which states, when the student is ready the teacher appears. When a student hears the material with an open mind and heart, it literally turns his world up-side-down. The reason is that the teachings are about what is not the truth more than the truth. As the student works with the information, layer after layer of old beliefs and judgments disintegrates. The automatic operations and reactions of the mind and body begin to be experienced more objectively, with less and less identification with them as being "I." This new way of experiencing living begins to bring a level of agape never before comprehended. As one discovers that he doesn't know, that the vain self is not the doer, that life is a game rather than a battle, that what we call goodness is greed, love is need, humility is vanity, worship is heavenly horse-trading, such things as problems, burdens and frustrations cease to exist as such. One finds that he is giving up nothing but his chains. With the decline of the knowledge of good and evil, there begins to be a simple awe and reverence for the essence of life. Christ takes on an entirely new meaning, one that is seen not as a conclusion but as a frame of reference, a demonstration, or as Werner says, an abstraction. This leads to the possibility of the transformation and regeneration, the fourth level of truth.

Please remember, the third level does not teach truth. It is a process of discovering what is not the truth. Underlying it all are some notions. These are not taught as doctrines, facts or truths. They are not to be believed. They are ways of looking at life so that we can get in touch with our experience regarding such points of view.

There is something very subtle and remarkable which happens naturally when the mind, with all of its smartness, gets "blown" away. A person begins pay-ing attention to what he does know, and that is what he experiences—with no explanations. One discovers that he has really never lived at "home." His attention was always out there someplace, with all his pre-conceived ideas about the past, the future, ultimate reality and contrived purposes. Such a thing as "living in the now," which was held in the mind as an ideal, just takes care of itself.

Without the "mind" claiming to be "I," one finds that all that is left is the self and what the self is is the source, creator, originator of experience. That is not a theory, a belief or even a notion. It is merely observed. Life functioning as "I" is observed, rather awesomely. It is the experience of being the context, being the space around which the whole panorama of the experience takes place.

Along this path one backs away from all the pre-conceived knowledge of God. In the awe and reverence to the new-found miracle of "being alive," being "source," one moves away from any belief in or about God to a sense of experience. The whole cosmos seems to be this same miracle, that what is happening "here" is also "there"—everywhere. It is rather natural, one finds, to see that ultimate and infinite SOURCE is indivisible and yet dividable. It is like attention which we can divide a dozen or two ways, yet it is still us. What each of us is is an individual self with many, many attention centers in one total center, possibly in the pattern or image of the cosmic source we have called God.

During the "not knowing" stage of development, a person may move away from Christianity as a set of stories, beliefs and obligations. Then from the freshness and emptiness or space of seeing like a young child sees, a whole new meaning of Jesus Christ begins to be experienced. It no longer is Christ and I. It ALL is Christ and it all is I. Christ was one who knew completely who he was, and he told his disciples in so many ways that they too were God, even Sons of God.

Christ is a title, a name, which describes the nature of the one being named. The nature that is called Christ is one who is anointed, filled and manifesting the divine light. Light is Life. There is only one life. Everything else is effect. Life is Source. Living bodies are manifestations and individualized awareness centers of Source. The awareness center in the body of a man named Jesus was open, totally open. As such, he was consciously aware that HE had created all "reality." He had created the earth, moon and stars. He had created all of us—and was all of us. The INDIVISIBLE whole was merely being as the awareness center of his physical body. The Whole is the Father. The particular, being flesh, is the Son. We have put our own conclusions about a "father" to correspond to our earthly experience. Since we are separate, physical entities from our earthly parents, we "believe" that we are separate entities from Source. A whole new meaning of father and son comes into one's experience.

As one looks at creation, there is a realization that Self is that which is now and forever, never changing—ever changing, the Alpha and the Omega, the beginning and the end, never greater, never lesser—just is. Self is complete and everything being done is manifest as being complete. Creation—total effect—is the evidence of what has been chosen by Source, Self, Initiation—name it what you will. Call it the Ultimate Ground of Being or whatever. It is of no significance. It is the one, awesome realization of being alive and participating in something totally incomprehensible and absolutely and incredibly marvelous. To be living with this sense, not as an idea or a concept, but as an experience, is to be waking up, approaching being conscious, alive, anointed. This is to take upon oneself the very name, meaning nature, of Christ.

The "Father" is the total Ground of Being. The "Son" is the vehicle, the creative tool, called the Word. Words are the tools of expressing comprehension. Processes of creation are going on through vehicles, even as a word is a vehicle. So each of us is the creative Word without knowing it. "The light shineth in darkness and the darkness comprehended it not."

John, in his profound introduction of his Gospel, describes the undescribable:

"In the beginning was the Word and the Word was with God and the Word was God. The same was in the beginning with God. All things were made by him and without him was not anything made that was made. In him was life and the life WAS THE LIGHT OF MEN . . . He was in the world and the world was made by him and the world knew him not. He came unto his own and his own received him not. BUT AS MANY AS RECEIVED HIM TO THEM GAVE HE POWER TO BECOME THE SONS OF GOD, EVEN TO THEM THAT BELIEVE ON HIS NAME . . . AND OF HIS FULNESS HAVE ALL WE RECEIVED, AND GRACE FOR GRACE."[2]

Those are words of cosmic abstractions. It is the fulness that Jesus was sharing with us. His fulness was without beginning or ending. His fulness was that of Total Creator, individualized as the Son. He was the Way, the Truth and the Life. He was the Father and the Son.

So a man who knew who he was once walked the dusty streets of a back-country in the Roman Empire. He taught the multitudes about a better life. He taught his disciples about a greater power. Then he took upon himself, publicly, as his own manifestation of the will of the Father, all the responsibility for everything people wanted to criticize in creation. He took upon him all the sins of the world.

The night before he did that, he acknowledged to his disciples that as long as he remained with them, they would never accept the reality of their own source. They would always be second handed, letting him be the source and they the effect. With his leaving, the Light of Truth would become their teacher. Everything that is, is the TRUTH. Every bit of it is a witness of how Source works. The sun shines on everyone without pettiness. The rain falls on the grateful and ungrateful alike. Gravity pulls just as surely on the nice boy as it does the bully. Everything bears witness of the Way of Source, the good news of God.

It is in the name or nature of the Father, Son and Light of Truth that a person is born again, brought back from the dead, the darkness. No longer is there becoming, getting, holding, hurting, fighting, defending, judging, even trying—only BEING. Being, the Father, is complete. The Son is Being complete. The Holy Spirit is the complete manifestation or, as we might say, the perfect result.

During the period of the last ten years, I have sometimes endured and sometimes enjoyed the proc-

ess that one experiences in working with the material on this level of truth. Thanks to a stranger who
came along the way, my "knowledge" became less
and less and my amazement grew more and more. A
year ago I heard about est. The more I read, the more
impressed I was with how it fit into the third or
"up-side-down" level of truth. Then I went myself. I
was surprised and joyfully shocked. What was being
communicated in hours was much of what I had
found in years and then, in some cases, more. I was
surprised to find so much given, so clearly, so
rapidly. As for my own experience of the training, I
found a rapid acceleration of the process that had
been ALWAYS going on.

With these thoughts in mind, I would like to return
to the profound talk Werner Erhard gave in 1976 on
the Transformation of est. We have already quoted
his introduction. The second part has to do with being
complete rather than getting more, better and/or different.

In 1971, some people might have seen the est training as a
fad. Or maybe it was a really good thing and would stay
around for a long time, like Dale Carnegie. It's gotten to be
fairly clear since then that est is not a fad—that it isn't even
another good idea that persists—that, in fact, it is unique. I
didn't say better. I just said unique.

est's uniqueness is related to the fact that the therapists
who have been through the training are nurtured by doing
therapy, the teachers are nurtured by teaching, and the
people who are going to school as students are nurtured by
being students. In fact, no matter what you do after the
training, you can be nurtured. When what your life is about
shifts from trying to get satisfied to BEING satisfied, then
ANY content (any thing in your life) is satisfying, nurturing,
and complete. So est isn't about improving the content of

one's life—it isn't about "getting better," though you may
have the experience of getting better. It's about shifting the
context in which all the events occur.

est's purpose is to create the space in which you can get
that your self is context rather than content—which enables
you to CREATE the story of your life rather than BE the
story or the events. So that everything becomes the completion of your transformation . . . That's what it is to be truly
transformed. It is to be in the space of "being transformed,"
so everything is transforming.

I want to be clear with you that est and transformation are
NOT a matter of getting better. I support things that make
people better; I support things that contribute to the content
of people's lives. But est is not about getting better. est is
about transformation.

In transformation, the self IS complete (the self as the self)
and the self is BEING COMPLETE. That is, a self that IS
complete manifests or expresses itself by BEING COM-
PLETE. That's important to get. A self that is complete
manifests or expresses itself by being complete. The context
is, IS COMPLETE—and the content is, BEING COM-
PLETE, BEING COMPLETE, BEING COMPLETE, etc.
The set is, IS COMPLETE—and the elements of the set are,
BEING COMPLETE, BEING COMPLETE, BEING
COMPLETE, and so on.[3]

Jesus testified that he and the Father were completely ONE. The Father IS COMPLETE and the
Son is the manifestation of the Father, which is
BEING COMPLETE, BEING COMPLETE.
Jesus' purpose was to share his own experience
which could reveal the complete duplicate of his
nature in all who would receive his demonstration.

This was the Way. Down through the ages of time
there have been other rare individuals who evolved
out of their sleep and shared the way of enlightenment. There is no need to compare any of these as to

which is greater, since they are all the One, being complete.

So in transformation, the context of one's life is that one IS complete, and the content of one's life, what it is about, is a process of BEING COMPLETE. So a transformation that's stopped, that doesn't express itself, that doesn't manifest itself, that isn't BEING COMPLETE, wasn't a transformation in the first place—it was at best a peak experience.

It is clear that people who think that transformation leads to narcissism and cuts you off from other people are confusing the "self" with a position, a body, an ego, an individual. The true experience of the self takes you out into the world to express the self.

If I had not shared the transformation which "occurred" five years ago it would not have been transformation. (After it "occurred" I could see that it always was—that it just is.) Not sharing it would have meant it was not true transformation. When I say "complete," I don't mean "over" or "finished" or "ended." If you are COMPLETE you are also always beginning at the same time. What I mean by "complete" is whole, fulfilled, entire, having all of the parts necessary to its integrity.

Remember the "Be-Do-Have" from the training? Well, in those terms one might say that transformation exists on the level of "being" and it manifests itself on the level of "doing" or process (completing itself), which results in "having" it. You manifest it (give it form) by completing it continually. If you complete it continually you have it and have always had it . . .[4]

The manifestation of Infinite Self or Being as taught in the New Testament is called the Godhead—the Father, the Word or Son and the Holy Spirit or Light of Truth. These three correspond to the way Werner describes the Be-Do-Have of being as follows:

Be   =   Father . . . .   The essence of Being

Do   =   Son . . . .   The aspect of creating or doing

Have = Spirit of Truth . . . The reality of creation, the per-
                                   fect revealed and materialized
                                   Light or energy of God, called
                                   "what is" or having.

Christ said that his real work was to enable people to be born again into the Kingdom of God, which was at hand. He said that the Kingdom of God is within us. He told his disciples to heal the sick and say to them, "The Kingdom of God has come NIGH unto you."

How would you define the Kingdom of God? Could we say that the kingdom was a state of joy, peace and love? What is joy? Joy is when everything is perfect just the way it is, right? What is peace? Peace is when we are not in conflict with what is. What is love, agape? It is totally accepting everything that is, just the way it is and just the way it is not. The only way living can be experienced as the Kingdom of God in joy, love and peace is to discover that everything, including the self, IS COMPLETE, wanting nothing.

The Kingdom of Heaven is a totally up-side-down world for the carnal man. One cannot make the world of opposites better and better until it is complete. One must really die to that world and be born again to a new world, the world of truth, the Spiritual World.

When one of the Jewish leaders, Nicodemus, came to Jesus by night, he was convinced that this strange young man was something very special. I would like to quote the way John the Beloved tells of the encounter. It is a beautiful summary of the meaning of Christ.

> Nicodemus . . . came to Jesus by night and said unto him, "Rabbi, we know that thou art a teacher come from God, for no man can do these miracles that thou doest, except God be with him."
>
> Jesus answered and said unto him, "Verily, verily, I say unto thee, Except a man be born again, he cannot see the kingdom of God."
>
> Nicodemus saith unto him, "How can a man be born when he is old? Can he enter the second time into his mother's womb and be born?"
>
> Jesus answered, "Verily, verily, I say unto thee, Except a man be born of water and of the Spirit, he cannot enter into the kingdom of God. That which is born of the flesh is flesh; and that which is born of the Spirit is spirit. Marvel not that I said unto thee, Ye must be born again. The wind bloweth where it listeth, and thou hearest the sound thereof, but canst not tell whence it cometh, and whither it goeth; so is every one that is born of the Spirit."
>
> Nicodemus answered and said unto him, "How can these things be?"
>
> Jesus answered and said unto him, "Art thou a master of Israel and knowest not these things? Verily, verily, I say unto thee, We speak that we do know and testify that we have seen (experienced) and ye receive not our witness. If I have told you of earthly things and ye believe not, how shall ye believe if I tell you of heavenly things? And no man hath ascended up to heaven but he that came down from heaven, even the Son of man WHICH IS IN HEAVEN."[5]

Nicodemus was living in heaven and had no way of seeing it.

---

1. Acts 1:3
2. John 1:1-16
3. Graduate Review, Nov., 1976
4. Ibid.
5. John 3:1-13

CHAPTER 11

The Game of Finding Out Who We Are

During World War II, I spent some time in India. It was an interesting and broadening experience. The many extremes, cultural and religious differences and the magnitude of the place brought about a personal experience in awareness which I have never forgotten. As I was watching masses of intent and preoccupied individuals, I got a strange illumination. I could see how God could create billions of people just like billions of ants, but how could one—just one—of them become "me?" What was it that made this one "me" and what is this "me" that I realize I am? It was my deepest experience up to that time of the "not know" mind.

I was fascinated with the sincerity and the complexity of the Hindu religion, just as I was later to enjoy visiting the Buddhist centers in China. I enjoyed visiting with the few I met who knew the deeper meaning behind all the outside trappings of their faiths. Just as Werner described his talks with the enlightened leaders of Buddhism, it is clear that the essence of those faiths are the same as the hidden teachings of Christianity.

In this chapter I want to deal with some of the hidden Hindu knowledge of enlightenment. The most popular writer on the Vedanta for Western readers was the late Alan W. Watts. One of his most intriguing books is *The Book—On the Taboo Against Knowing Who You Are*. He relates one of the old oriental stories. Although it has been seven years since I first read it, the impact of the story has remained with me ever since.

As part of the setting for the story, I will include some of his material leading up to it.

We do not need a new religion or a new bible. We need a new experience—a new feeling of what is to be "I." The lowdown (which is, of course, the secret and profound view) on life is that our normal sensation of self is a hoax or, at best, a temporary role that we are playing, or have been conned into playing—with our own tacit consent, just as every hypnotized person is basically willing to be hypnotized. The most strongly enforced of all known taboos is the taboo against knowing who or what you really are behind the mask of your apparently separate, independent, and isolated ego . . .

The difficulty in realizing this to be so is that conceptual thinking cannot grasp it. It is as if the eyes were trying to look at themselves directly, or as if one were trying to describe the color of a mirror in terms of colors reflected in the mirror. Just as sight is something more than all things seen, the foundation or "ground" of our existence and our awareness cannot be understood in terms of things that are known. We are forced, therefore, to speak of it through myth—that is, through special metaphors, analogies, and images which say what it is LIKE as distinct from what it IS. At one extreme of its meaning, "myth" is fable, falsehood, or superstition. But at another, "myth" is a useful and fruitful image by which we make sense of life in somewhat the same way that we can explain electrical forces by comparing them with behavior of water or air. Yet "myth," in this second sense, is not to be taken literally, just as electricity is not to be confused with air or water. Thus in using myth one must take care not to confuse image with fact, which would be like climbing up the signpost instead of following the road.

Myth, then, is the form in which I try to answer when children ask me those fundamental metaphysical questions which come so readily to their minds: "Where did the world come from?'' ''Why did God make the world?'' Where was I before I was born?'' ''Where do people go when they die?'' Again and again I have found that they seem to be satisified with a simple and very ancient story, which goes something like this:

There was never a time when the world began, because it goes round and round like a circle, and there is no place on a circle where it begins. Look at my watch, which tells the time; it goes round, and so the world repeats itself again and again. But just as the hour-hand of the watch goes up to twelve and down to six, so, too, there is day and night, waking and sleeping, living and dying, summer and winter. You can't have any one of these without the other, because you wouldn't be able to know what black is unless you had seen it side-by-side with white, or white unless side-by-side with black.

. . . It's also like the game of hide-and-seek, because it's always fun to find new ways of hiding, and to seek for someone who doesn't always hide in the same place.

God also likes to play hide-and-seek, but because there is nothing outside God, he has no one but himself to play with. But he gets over this difficulty by pretending that he is not himself. This is his way of hiding from himself. He pretends that he is you and I and all the people in the world, all the animals, all the plants, all the rocks, and all the stars. In this way he has strange and wonderful adventures, some of which are terrible and frightening. But these are just like bad dreams, for when he wakes up they will disappear.

Now when God plays hide and pretends that he is you and I, he does it so well that it takes him a long time to remember where and how he hid himself. But that's the whole fun of it—just what he wanted to do. He doesn't want to find himself too quickly, for that would spoil the game. That is why it is so difficult for you and me to find out that we are God in disguise, pretending not to be himself. But when the game has gone on long enough, all of us will wake up, stop pretending, and remember that we are all one single Self—the God who is all that there is and who lives for ever and ever.

Of course, you must remember that God isn't shaped like a person. People have skins and there is always something outside our skins. If there weren't we wouldn't know the difference between what is inside and outside our bodies. But God has no skin and no shape because there isn't any outside to him. The inside and the outside of God are the same. And though I have been talking about God as 'he' and not 'she,' God isn't a man or a woman, I didn't say 'it' because we usually say 'it' for things that aren't alive.

God is the Self of the world, but you can't see God for the same reason that, without a mirror, you can't see your own eyes, and you certainly can't bite your own teeth or look inside your head. Your self is that cleverly hidden because it is God hiding.

You may ask why God sometimes hides in the form of horrible people, or pretends to be people who suffer great disease and pain. Remember, first, that he isn't really doing this to anyone but himself. Remember , too, that in almost all the stories you enjoy there have to be bad people as well as good people, for the thrill of the tale is to find out how the good people will get the better of the bad. It's the same as when we play cards. At the beginning of the game we shuffle them all into a mess, which is like the bad things in the world, but the point of the game is to put the mess into good order, and the one who does it best is the winner. Then we shuffle the cards once more and play again, and so it goes with the world.

This story, obviously mythical in form, is not given as a *scientific* description of the way things are. Based on the analogies of games and the drama, and using that much worn-out word "God" for the Player, the story claims only to be LIKE the way things are. I use it just as astronomers use the image of inflating a black balloon with white spots on it for the galaxies, to explain the expanding universe. But to most children, and many adults, the myth is at once intelligible, simple, and fascinating . . . .

"The Ultimate Ground of Being" is Paul Tillich's decontaminated term for "God" and would also do for "the Self of the world" as I put it in my story for children. But the secret which my story slips over to the child is that the Ultimate Ground of Being is you. Not of course, the everyday you which the Ground is assuming, or "pretending" to be, but that inmost Self which escapes inspection because it's always the inspector. This, then, is the taboo of taboos: you're IT!

Yet in our culture this is the touchstone of insanity, the blackest of blasphemies, and the wildest of delusions. This, we believe, is the ultimate in megalomania—an inflation of the ego to complete absurdity. For though we cultivate the ego with one hand, we knock it down with the other. From generation to generation we kick the stuffing out of our children to teach them to "know their place" and to behave, think and feel with proper modesty as befits one little ego among many. As my mother used to say, "You're not the only pebble on the beach!" Any one in his right mind who believes that he is God should be crucified or burned at the stake, though now we take the more charitable view that no one in his right mind could believe such nonsense. Only a poor idiot could conceive himself as the omnipotent ruler of the world, and expect everyone else to fall down and worship.

But this is because we think of God as the King of the Universe, the Absolute Technocrat who personally and consciously controls every detail of his cosmos—and that is not the kind of God in my story. In fact, it isn't MY story at all, for any student of the history of religions will know that it comes from ancient India, and is the mythical way of explaining the Vedanta philosophy. Vedanta is the teaching of the Upanishads, a collection of dialogues, stories and poems, most of which go back to at least 800 B.C. Sophisticated Hindus do not think of God as a special and separate superperson who RULES the world from above, like a monarch. Their God is "underneath" rather than "above" everything, and he (or it) PLAYS the world from inside . . .

But Vedanta is much more than the idea or the belief that this is so. It is centrally and above all the EXPERIENCE, the immediate knowledge of its being so, and for this reason such a complete subversion of our ordinary way of seeing things . . .

Furthermore, on seeing through the illusion of the ego, it is impossible to think of oneself as better than, or superior to, others for having done so. In every direction there is just the one Self playing its myriad games of hide-and-seek. Birds are not better than the eggs from which they have broken. Indeed, it could be said that a bird is one egg's way of becoming other eggs. Egg is ego, and bird is the liberated Self.[1]

I trust that the above contribution by Alan Watts was as stimulating to you as it has been to me. It is so difficult for the Western mind to grasp the possibly deeper view of seeing the wholeness—holiness in the New Testament—of life. Werner Erhard also has some interesting observations on how the East can assist us to grasp wholes. He made this statement regarding a question as to whether est teaches Eastern thought.

Each person ought to contribute whateve he or she has, and I have a particular approach which I think makes some contribution, and the approach is one of wanting to get the universal from the Eastern tradition, rather than wanting to be the EASTERN from the Eastern tradition. Part of my intention for est is to not allow it to become Western OR Eastern, but to keep its intention to be as universal as possible, so that it can contribute to whatever is valuable in the East as Eastern, and to whatever is valuable in the West as Western.

You know, Eastern spirituality sounds illogical sometimes when Western logic tries to apprehend it. But Western logic has now come into a new era, recognizing that there's a logic that applies to wholes which is distinct and different from the logic that applies to parts . . .

I guess the simplest model I have . . . is one of throwing a ball up in the air. In this analogy, you have the hand as home base, or the original nature of things, or the way it all is. When you throw the ball up into the air, it appears that it's getting farther and farther away from your hand. Then there's a place at the top where it's going neither up nor down. That would be, for me what's called "transformation," after which it begins to return home, to the hand.

If you step back from that whole process, you can see that when the ball is going up, it's actually returning to the hand, because it's approaching transformation. It's approaching that state in which it's going neither up nor down. And it obviously has to expend all the energy inherent in itself going AWAY from the hand before it can go BACK to the hand.

So the whole trip AWAY from the hand is really toward the hand—if you just stand back far enough to see the entire process . . . The point that I want to make is that people don't have to sweat about or worry over whether it's all going to turn out. For me, tranformation really is the experience that it not only IS going to turn out, it already HAS turned out . . .

You know, people are trying to "get satisfied," or "become enlightened," or to do something to achieve enlightenment, all of which is funadmentally inconsistent with enlightenment. If enlightenment is the natural state of self, and since you obviously couldn't be anything but yourself, you are obviously already enlightened. You may be in that part of enlightenment that is going AWAY from the hand, and that's a part of being enlightened. It's not wrong to be unenlightened—to be unenlightened is part of being enlightened.[2]

---

1. From *The Book: On the Taboo Against Knowing Who You Are*, by Alan Watts. Copyright 1966 by Alan Watts. Pages 9-19. Reprinted by permission of Pantheon Books, a Division of Random House, Inc.
2. Graduate Review, April 1977, pp. 5-7.

CHAPTER 12

The Way of the Church

Ever since its beginning, Christianity has been committed to a church orientation. One way or another, whenever people have accepted Christ in a different way than the churches around them, they got themselves organized into a new church. According to Christian theology, the church serves as a religious family, presided over by a paternal shepherd, the unity of the group forming a protection against the non-believers on the outside. Loyalty to Christ meant loyalty to the church institution.

My intention in this chapter is to discuss the difference in function and value of the church as it appears on the four levels of truth. On the obedience level, it is the Kingdom of God, with Christ as the head. Its divine authority to bless and to withhold blessings is to carry over into the next life. On the faith level, the church is seen as a mystical body of Christ rather than just a specific organization. Thus church service and loyalty become less sectarian and more symbolic of one's commitment to the Lord. On the third or understanding level, the institution becomes incidental to the process of self-discovery. It is like the cocoon stage between caterpillar and butterfly. In this stage, the teaching is on a one-to-one basis as master and student and not so much one of organization. This does not mean that a person would not remain functional in church service. It is only that such activity is incidental to the process of discovering the personal illusions which make up the barriers to illumination. Just as the disciples spent this period of forty days without preaching or other "constructive" activity, so might a person who experienced an 180 degree about-face. Then, on the fourth level after the anointing, the church is no longer seen as something to be served in order to get something. Instead, the church becomes a very valuable instrument to be used. It becomes a form of cohesive, cooperative activity which enables those "who are perfect" to support the efforts of each other as well as those on other levels, working on projects of value to humanity.

Since most Christians have only experienced the obedience level, the church has usually been recognized as the single access to the salvation of Christ. It is believed that since the church is the Kingdom of God on the earth, if one is out of harmony with it here, he will certainly be out of harmony with it in the eternal world. Thus the church leaders have felt the heavy responsibility of protecting and defending the church. In such belief, the church becomes the presence of Christ on earth and will be exalted as the Kingdom of God in the eternities to come.

It will be surprising, then, for most people to hear that Paul, the great proponent of the church, made it clear that it was designed as a temporary vehicle to keep the flock together only until the process of perfection had been accomplished in the lives of the members. At such a time there would be no further need for the authoritative structure of the church since all would be secure in their own light.

Paul stated this concept of the church in a letter to the members in Ephesus: "And he (Jesus) gave some apostles and some prophets and some evangelists and some pastors and teachers (the founding organization of the church) FOR THE PERFECTING OF THE SAINTS, for the work of the ministry, for the edifying of the body of Christ, *TILL* WE ALL COME IN THE UNITY OF THE FAITH AND OF THE KNOWLEDGE OF THE SON OF GOD, UNTO A PERFECT MAN, unto the measure of the stature of the FULNESS OF CHRIST. That we henceforth be no more children tossed to and fro and carried about with every wind of doctrine, by the sleight of men and cunning craftiness whereby they lie in wait to deceive."[1]

So as Paul describes it here, the church was designed to protect the "babes in Christ" during their uncertain period until the members were transformed into the perfect fulness of Christ. Since Paul had personally experienced illumination, he knew that when the members had experienced their own transformation, they too would need no teachers. John had declared exactly that. Let me quote it again: "But the anointing which ye have received of him abideth in you and ye need not that ANY MAN TEACH YOU, but as the same anointing teacheth you of all things, and is truth and is no lie, and even as it hath taught you, ye shall abide in him."[2]

In other words, the church as a structured and authoritative body was to put itself out of business. Undoubtedly there still would be the church, but it seems that by necessity it would be a very different kind of organization than the one designed to protect everyone from false leaders and strange doctrines. Possibly the church would be one of cooperating equals who would function harmoniously in joint

ventures. There would be no requirement or necessity to do so, just the opportunities such a group
provides to do things together.

The history of the Christian Church shows that
Paul's dream was never realized. It has been said that
power corrupts and absolute power corrupts absolutely. The difficulties of power were being violently
manifest even during the first generation when the
apostolic leadership was trying diligently to keep the
"saints" from tearing the church apart. Since the
majority of the members never went beyond the first
two levels, the next generation was almost totally on
the first level. They admit in their writings that they
were not experiencing the miraculous gifts. In church
history, these dedicated second generation leaders are
called the apologists since they no longer had the
power themselves but testified that their predecessors
had experienced it.

For two thousand years now, the church has been
accepted as permanent. Since "perfection" to the
carnal man is unattainable in this life, it appeared that
the church would be indispensable until the Second
Coming of the Lord. Then too, the Second Coming
was seen as a literal event, which was always just
around the corner, when Jesus was to purify and
cleanse the faithful from their carnal nature. As long
as a church is bitterly persecuted, the great sacrifices
required of all members build great inner strength.
Yet when the persecution turns to public acceptance,
rivalries and controversies turn member against
member. Dogmatism, bigotry, superstition and other
forms of "the knowledge of good and evil" turned
Christian Europe into a millennium of gross darkness.

We pour much money and effort into the support of our various churches with the hope that they will some day be able to do the job that has not yet been done in two thousand years. There is a reason why the church has failed. Since every church is dedicated to the knowledge of good and evil, it must divide. Every church is founded on the claim that it has the one good that all can accept and be united together, so it just polarizes another division. As Paul pled in dismay, "There should be no schism in the body, but that the members should have the same care one for another."[3]

It is the old story—love unites and fear divides. The mind of right and wrong is fearful and finds security and comfort in joining with those who agree. We live by and for agreement. We fear those who do not agree with us and think we love those who believe like we do. We have nice descriptions for those who give us agreement, such as the faithful, loyal, dedicated, patriotic, trustworthy, religious and bright.

Since agreement is an invisible and transient point of view, we find ways of making it more visible and permanent. We attach it to symbols and then take comfort that others also respect the symbols. But most of all we organize it. We get together, give our agreements a name, make up rules and establish authority for control. As the beliefs are identified with good, those who disagree are seen as bad. Feelings of competition, fear, suspicion and disgust begin to separate us from the disbelievers. As competition between groups increases, violence of various kinds occurs when one collides with the other. This violence is given civilized names like argumentation (called defending the truth), boycott (called not supporting your enemy), pirating (called giving part of the enemy a chance to be right), strike (called refusing to be exploited), law suit (called trying to get justice), divorce (called solving a problem) and war (called defending the peace). All these are really the violence of agreement in opposition to disagreement.

I am not saying there is anything wrong with organizations and institutions, whether they be a government, army, religion, business, school or family. It is that they become sources of competition because we depend upon them to protect us from what we fear. In our fear of being wrong and our need to be right, we identify with the group with which we can agree. What we agree with is generally based upon the conditioning we received from those we accept as our authorities. Different authorities—different agreements. Then through identification, we become a part of something bigger than ourselves. In the scriptures, Paul calls these supreme entities to which we give our loyalties our "principalities," the place of the prince. These become the bastions of the collective double mind and the entrenched enemy of liberation. As Paul described his losing battle against vortexes of competition: "For we wrestle not against flesh and blood, but against PRINCIPALITIES, against POWERS, against the rulers of the DARKNESS OF THIS WORLD, AGAINST SPIRITUAL WICKEDNESS IN HIGH PLACES."[4]

Not only was this his indictment of the established churches and institutions of his day, it became true within the new church itself. It is for this reason that most of the teachers of the hidden wisdom have never "gotten organized" and never tried to "mass produce" enlightenment. Every attempt to do so has failed to produce liberation and has produced "believers" instead. Since all mass eduction, whether secular or religious, has come through our principalities, little information has been available to us about the existence of such "wisemen." Yet there is considerable evidence that they have been around, keeping certain ideas alive and working with a student here and another there. They have neither sought nor desired agreement. They have felt no need to change the world, for the world was exactly the way it was because of what it was. When the curious have sought signs and wonders, the men of power have not obliged. When the seekers have sought "truth," the teachers have minded their own business. But when someone came asking, not out of belief or disbelief, not out of a need to prove or disprove, but out of the awe of not knowing, they have been there to show a direction and to ask the appropriate questions that would set them free.

Much of their material has been widely published but since it is concealed behind outer pretenses, many of us have not taken the time to look for the hidden meanings. One of the old "outer appearances" was alchemy, supposedly turning base metal into gold but actually turning carnal man into spiritual man. Another safe disguise was astrology. The twelve signs of the Zodiac are far more than for fortune telling. They describe the twelve ages in which mankind is evolving forward towards our ultimate spiritual potential. Each age is approximately two thousand years in length. Since we are concluding the age commenced by Christ and beginning the so-called Age of Aquarius, it might be well to give some thought to the information. Remember, this material is of value as notions.

Six thousand years ago was the beginning of the Age of Taurus, the Bull. Its beginning was heralded by a perfect man whose name was Enoch, who "walked with God and he was not, for God took him."[5] Many people think that the next age which started around four thousand years ago, the Age of Aries, the Ram, was brought in by the father of the Israelites, Abraham. Actually, Abraham was a student of the great teacher and perfect man, Melchisedec. He was king of Salem, which means king of righteousness and peace. Paul says of him that he was "made like unto the Son of God" and was a "priest of the Most High God," which means that he was a man who had the fulness of the POWER OF GOD. Tradition says that both Enoch and Melchisedec perfected the people in their cities and both populations were translated to a higher sphere. The city of Jerusalem—the "New" Salem—was built on the site where Melchisedec's city of Salem stood.

The Age of Aries was put into operation by Abraham's grandson, Jacob (changed to Israel) and his twelve sons. This was a massive, long range plan to see if the teachings could be institutionalized for mass-production through a nation that was made up of one family, the twelve tribes of the family of Israel. Its teachings were designed to reveal the great truth that God is One, infinite and eternal. It raised man to a very high level of the literal law of obedience. God was revealed to the masses for the first time as a God of Justice. The ram, a male sheep, has to do with a flock and the shepherd. Abraham and his descendents were primarily shepherds.

The world went through many changes during the two thousand years that followed. Toward the end, the basis for the next age was set by the phenomenon of a stable world power, the Roman Empire. This was the beginning of the Age of Pisces, the Fish. The teachings would now be taken beyond the flock to the world, as a net is cast into the sea. In fact the early Christian symbol for Christianity was a fish. The cross was not a popular symbol until long after. It would be like us glorifying the electric chair if it was used to execute our hero.

Paul, who had made the painful transition from the old teachings to the new, wanted to make it very clear to his Jewish cousins that the previous age had been replaced by a new day. The Law of Moses and its Levitical Priesthood were only preparatory steps to the higher Truth. He stressed that for this new age there would have to be another *teacher like Melchisedec*: "And it is yet far more evident, for that after the similitude of Melchisedec there ARISETH ANOTHER PRIEST, who is made, not after the law of a carnal commandment (for the natural man) but after the POWER OF AN ENDLESS LIFE (for the spiritual man) . . . For the law made NOTHING PERFECT, but the bringing in of a better hope did, by the which we draw nigh unto God . . . If therefore PERFECTION were by the Levitical priesthood, for under it the people received the law, what further need was there that another priest should rise AFTER THE ORDER OF MELCHISEDEC and not be called after the order of Aaron? For the priesthood being changed, there is made of necessity a change also of the law."[6]

Jesus Christ became the great world teacher who

ushered in the great new revelation that God is love.
He too was caught up to heaven but he left twelve
special witnesses—most of whom were fishermen—to
become fishers of men. A new organization, a church,
was formed which would go beyond the family of
Israel, out to the four corners of the world. There
was to be no discretion according to race, status, sex
or slavery. It carried in its gospel net the great
revelation that God is Father and we are his children.

Yet, just as the theocratic institution of Israel had
become a ruthless principality, justifying everything
from indifference to holy warfare, so eventually did
the new church built by the twelve apostles. Christ's
seven proclamations of evil—ye scribes, Pharisees,
hypocrites—which he broadcast to the leaders of the
Jewish Church (Matt. 23) could and would soon be
leveled at the leaders of the church which would bear
his name. "So then because thou art lukewarm and
neither cold nor hot, I will spue thee out of my
mouth. Because thou sayest, I am rich and increased
with goods and have need of nothing; and knowest
not that thou are wretched and miserable and poor
and blind and naked."[7]

So now another age, the age of Pisces, has run its
course and a new age, another two thousand year
period has commenced. It is called the Age of
Aquarius, the Water Bearer. This has been spoken of
as the age of enlightenment when people all over the
world will discover who they are—not just the
created, not just heirs, but individualized presence of
Being, the Infinite Self, the creator and the created.

This giant, awesome leap for mankind has been in
the process of coming, it is said, in eleven ages,
covering the last twenty four thousand years. We

have been seeing the new age getting under way during the last hundred years. As was foretold, we are living at a time when the whole process of living on the earth is being revolutionized, including every science. Ninety-five percent of the engineers and scientists that have ever lived are living today. The marvels of a hundred years ago, such as the steamboat, railroad and telegraph have given way to the automobile, airplane, jets, rockets, telephone, radio, movies, recordings, television, communication satellites, plastics, wonder-drugs, atomic energy and on and on. Probably more revolutionary than all of them is the computer, and we have only been into that for thirty years.

As in each age of the past, it is going to be a completely new chapter in the history of mankind, yet even more dramatic than those of the past. As a matter of fact, we are, in our own generation, experiencing the obvious beginning of a change in everything in the outer world around us. Our political, social and ecclesiastical institutions, our methods of doing our daily work, our relationship with one another, our manifold instruments of self-expression and self-discovery—are all undergoing a radical change and for the better.

However, all of these things, in and of themselves, do not herald the change. Most significantly, during all of this, is what has been happening to the way people think. In the year 1600, Francis Bacon became the father of modern science because he wrote stories which encouraged people to start looking at things "without knowing." That seemingly obvious "point of view" is the key to scientific research, yet the world was stagnant for hundreds of years because it was considered blasphemous to suggest that all knowledge was not already known.

As all of us have unknowingly stretched our awareness to grasp things like the speed of light, relativity, and expanding universe, atomic particles, DNA and RNA, instant replay and microwave cooking, the cosmic awesomeness of life itself begins to come nearer the surface. The Aquarian Age is to be the age of personal freedom. True freedom is an inner state of being which comes from knowing who one is, which comes from knowing God. Each age brings man to a higher revelation of his source. This age is the age of the Man with the Water Pot ("Seek ye a man bearing a pot of water"). Who is the man with the water pot? Why, the Gardener, of course. So the symbol of this new age is to be the Gardener. Man, having graduated as Shepherd and as a Fisherman, now becomes a Gardener. That is a title which wonderfully describes the new role of man who is already unlocking the mysteries of inner and outer space, unleashing the power of the atom, harnessing the presence of cosmic frequencies, delving into the building blocks of living cells, and on and on.

But the greatest change is coming by being a Gardener at the Tree of Life where we rediscover not so much the Garden of Eden as the Garden of Being. The secret of being is that one is always beginning and never ending, yet always complete. Man is being driven to this by the broken promises of the Tree of Knowledge of Good and Evil. That false knowledge has always assured him that he would be happy if he just had plenty to eat, comfortable facilities, adequate education, frequent entertainment, abundant pleasures and secure borders. These were the ideals he could only dream about in past centuries but has now obtained. And do you know what? He is still not happy! There is still no fulness of joy, no great inner peace, no perfect love that has no fear. Where does one go when he finds he has been ripped off?

At this stage the question naturally presents itself—Who is, or who is to be, the great teacher and prophet of our new Aquarian Age? Well, it seems that there is no lack of candidates for the position. All over the world interesting people are laying claim to this high office, or their followers are claiming it for them. It may just be, in this particular age, after all these thousands of years of upward striving, we may have reached the stage where humanity is ready to do without personal prophets of any kind and to contact the Living God at first hand. Never until now has this been possible for the great majority. But now, chiefly owing to the work that has been done in the race-mind by those illuminated beings who have preceded us, it has become possible for all men and women to move beyond the mind and body to discover the true self.

So it may just be that the "Great World Teacher" of the New Age is not to be any man or woman, or any textbook, or any organization, but the Spirit of Truth which each individual is to find and contact for himself. Only recently has a vast number of humanity become capable of using the "abstract mind," the true self. It is still quite true, of course, that precious few ever use it yet, but at least most could if they wanted to.

---

1. Ephesians 4:10-14
2. I John 2:27
3. I Cor 12:25
4. Eph. 6:12
5. Genesis 5:24
6. Heb. 7:3-19
7. Revelations 3:15-17

CHAPTER 13
The Organizing of est

As we have seen in the previous chapter, the double mind identifies with an institution as a super-self, the place of the prince, called a principality. Since I had been aware of this danger to the higher teachings for quite some time, I wondered how Werner Erhard could be using an organization to mass produce third level instruction. As far as I had been able to find, it had never worked before.

What I found was that Werner knew the danger of principalities as well, if not better, than I did. In his years of searching he had seen little else. When transformation came, it was not the result of any group, doctrine, system or even a teacher. He experienced enlightenment the only way it can come, as an individual, on the level of INDIVIDUALITY. Like many before him, Werner wanted to share it. He even wanted to mass produce it. Yet he was aware of the delicate line between liberation and captivation, conversion and inversion, refining and defining, relieving and believing.

With his "not knowing" mind he ran experiments. He put together the training and it worked. Every month since, the training is examined to see what is and what is not working lately. As a larger and larger organization was required, more experiments were run. Werner began to focus on a very revolutionary notion that there is a transformation of self beyond individuality, on the level of RELATIONSHIP. He also saw that beyond relationship was another level,

which was transformation on the level of INSTITU-
TION. Whether these were new abstractions to him
or old ideas whose time had come, I do not know.
But to Werner, they opened the door to the possibil-
ity , even probability, for the transformation of SO-
CIETY.

When I experienced the training, I found it hard to
believe it was happening. This was mass-production
and it was working, as far as I could tell. I remem-
bered what had been said about the Age of Aquarius
being the age of enlightenment. Could this be a part
of it? Could it be that what had never before been
able to work would be able to work now? Don't you
believe it! Believing one way or another is totally
irrelevant. Getting in touch with one's experience of
it is all that can work anyway. If it works, it works.

One thing we can be very certain about is that
regardless of what est is, graduates can make a "principality" out of it. They can believe in it, identify
with it, make it their authority, promote it, defend it
and serve it. And that is okay. They get the booby
prize. For them est works for getting better, not for
transformation. Werner does not want graduates to
do any of the above. He only wants them to USE est.
So for those who relate to est, not as effect, but as
cause, Werner is inviting them to experience not just
one transformation, but three—on the levels of individuality, relationship and institution. So let us take a
look at them one at a time.

What is meant by transformation on the level of
individuality? The word "individual" means UNdivided. Look in the dictionary to see the definition for
yourself. Most people seem to think that it means the
exact opposite. It suggests separateness to them, but

they are mistaken. Individual means undivided. Infinite Self has the power of individualizing Self without, so to speak, breaking Self into parts. As we
discussed in the game of hide and seek, God indi-
vidualizes Self as man, and so each of us is an
individualization of God. God can individualize Self
in an infinite number of distinct beings, or units of
consciousness, and yet not be in any way separate.
Only Life can do this. Matter cannot be individualized. It can only be broken up. Since our cus-
tomary training prepares us to understand only matter, this is a totally new idea to most people.

So our real self, the Christ aspect, the spiritual
man, the "I Am," is an individualization of God. WE
ARE THE PRESENCE OF GOD AT THE
POINT WHERE WE ARE. So Divine Mind, Self,
becomes self-conscious in YOU, ME, THEM. To
directly experience this re-awakening of self is to be a
totally different life, based on *IN*dividuality rather
than *CON*dividuality. Condividuality is seeing oneself as a separate entity WITH all other separate
entities.

Now, what is meant by transformation on the level
of relationship? What Werner had to say about it at
his talk on the transformation of est is fairly heavy
reading, yet it might be the best place to start:

> We are not talking about INDIVIDUALS OR A RELA-
> TIONSHIP. We are talking about the context for
> individuals—which is individuality, and the context for
> relationships—which is relationship. Both individuality and
> relationship are contexts—not contents.
>
> But what about the context of relationship? What is that?
> Actually, nobody's ever really gotten that far, so the self as
> self has never completed itself. Part of the reason for that is
> the ACTUAL interface between individuality, at one end of
> the spectrum, and society, at the other.

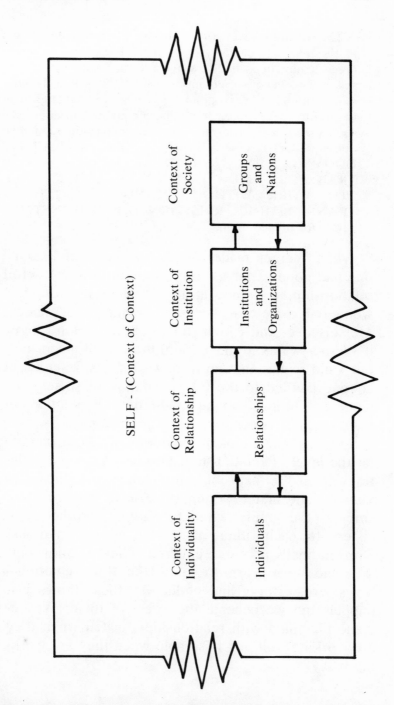

The self at the level of individuality interfaces with the self at the level of relationship (or family). Looking from the opposite direction—that is, moving toward individuality—the self at the level of society interfaces with the self at the level of institution (or organization). So you can see that individuality gets to society through relationship and organization, and society gets to individuality through organization and relationship. YOU CAN WORK FROM NOW UNTIL DOOMSDAY ON INDIVIDUALS TO CREATE A TRANSFORMATION IN SOCIETY AND IT WILL NOT WORK WITHOUT HANDLING—WITHOUT TRANSFORMING—RELATIONSHIP AND INSTITUTION (or organization).[1]

When Werner made the above statement that no one had gone as far as tranformation on the level of relationship, let alone at the level of institution, I wondered if he was accurate. What about Enoch, Melchisedec, and Christ, for example? I don't know if Werner wants to make them the exceptions or not, but I did realize that up to now no transformation of anyone has led to the transformation of society, let alone institutions, so he might have a point about even the in-between step of relationship.

So let us take a look at the notion of transformation on the level of relationship. Ordinary man sees relationship as "effect" of the "choice" by those involved. The first experience we have with relationships is the family; child to parents, brothers and sisters to each other, then marriage of man and woman, finally parent to children. These relationships are where we learn to know the three emotional loves: eros, storge and philia. All these things just happen and we become the effect of them. We become identified with relationships, elated when they are working well and miserable when they are working badly.

What the double mind does with a relationship is to try to get it to be completely right. As each additional relationship is established, it is an extension of "my family" and we begin to "need" these people for our lives to "feel" complete. A relationship develops a life of its own, its own knowledge of good/evil, right/wrong—all the opposites, including going-on/stopping, like living/dying. As relationships grow on agreements, ideals, duties and obligations, they become entanglements of compulsion and control. The clearest way to see the evil in our "carnal" relationships is the way we end them. We can't just say thank you and walk away. We have to find ways to excuse us for breaking off. We have to find all kinds of ways to make the other person wrong. We cancel their vote, saying, "Sheeesh! What a character. I think I knew it all along. What took me so long to see?" We have to make the other wrong so we can feel right about terminating the relationship.

Transformation on the level of relationship takes place when relationship is experienced as SOURCE rather than effect. The relationship, itself, becomes self—on another level other than self at the level of individuality. We might say it is self experienced in a compounding way. It is an expanded context. The relationship is a conscious union of multiple individuality, a joining of purpose which IS COMPLETE and manifests itself in BEING COMPLETE. The relationship IS—FOREVER, with continual starting and no ending. It is the experience of the space to be totally what one is and what one is not. In the space of that relationship, nothing can be seen as "bad."

Werner describes how this transformation took place with him through his relationship with est graduates.

. . . For some of you, your self is actually transformed or enlightened at the level of relationship. For me, that happened out of my relationship with the graduates. You created the space for a training that I went through. Can you imagine the kind of space that it gave me when . . . 80,000 people create a relationship with me that is complete? In that space, I went through a training of my self at the level of relationship (remember, when I get in touch with my self and you get in touch with your self, we will see the same self).

I hadn't even realized that the training of self at the level of relationship was complete. I had my intention on it, but not my attention. At any rate, someplace I got that my self (the self) was transformed at the level of relationship, that the self as relationship was complete, and that completion was also a beginning. And that set the stage for transformation of self at the level of institution.[2]

Werner would probably tell us that he never would have experienced transformation on the level of relationship if he had not experimented with an organization to take transformation into the world. That was started in 1972. The transformation of Werner on the level of organization occurred in 1976, four years later.

The story of what steps Werner took in putting an institution together is very revealing. He was not interested in creating a "church" where graduates would become loyal members. He was thinking only of organizing a working team. No one would "belong to" est. There might be only those who "worked at" est. Here is his story:

In order for the experience of transformation to be complete (to be true transformation), transformation ultimately would have to be taken out into the world, out where society and humanity can be transformed. So what?, one might say.

So what if we don't take the experience of transformation out into the world? What's the difference? . . . Well, the fact of the matter is that if you don't take it out into the world—if you don't continue to complete it—you didn't get it in the first place.

What I got clear about was that it should require an organization, an institution—and a particular kind of organization—to take the experience of transformation out into the world, into society. That which is complete would be complete by continuing to complete itself . . . And the way I would begin would be to learn what there was to know about organizations that work.

What I found out when I began to explore the subject of organizations was that there are no organizations and no institutions in the world—at least none that I have come in contact with—that work.

I want to define what it means for an organization to work. First of all, an organization that works remains true to its purpose. When you study organizations you find that almost every one of them loses its purpose very soon after it is organized. It becomes a mechanism, the purpose of which is persistence or survival or self-perpetuation.

In est, the organization's purpose is to serve people, to create an opportunity for people to experience transformation, enlightenment, satisfaction and well-being in their lives. And to create an opportunity for people to participate in making the world work and to contribute to the lives of others. That's the purpose of est.

The second criterion for an organization that works is that it be viable in the world. By viable I mean "workable," able to support and handle itself in the world—able to create the effects it intends, to get the job done.

And the third criterion for an organization that works is that it nurture the people who participate in it, to the degree that they choose to come in contact with it. So, an organization that works doesn't make them less than they are. Of course, most organizations do sacrifice people to the organization, and there is something fundamentally evil in that—evil in the sense of trading aliveness for survival.

As Werner started building an organization that would work, he continued to make discoveries. He found that professional management people like myself had our concepts of organizations up-side-down and inside-out. Since I have lectured nationally for many years on concepts of managerial operations, I thought I knew what made an organization work. I would list them in the following order:

1. Integrity: The dedication, commitment and loyalty of people.
2. Relationship: a clear chain of command, with everyone knowing the scope and skill of his job and who his boss is.
3. Communication: Knowing what is really going on above and below.
4. Responsibility: Knowing who is accountable and having them fix it when it goes wrong.

These four elements are very necessary for SUCCESS. They are also, unfortunately, the way we pay for survival by giving up aliveness. Werner discovered that you do not end with responsibility, you must start with it. He also found very different definitions—transforming concepts—for these four principles. Responsibility means being SOURCE. Communication means being AGAPE. Relationship means being SPACE. Integrity means being TRUTH. You start with responsibility—source—and end with integrity—truth. Here is the way Werner describes his discoveries:

> So back in 1972, I became clear that an organization that works is essential to completing transformation, and I set out to discover the elements you need to put into an organization to find out what could make it work.
> The first thing I found was that you need a thing called source—someone who is willing to be totally responsible. I

didn't say that source would make an organization work. I just knew that if you didn't have source you'd never find out what does make an organization work. Unless someone is willing to be totally responsible, everyone HAS to be responible, and responsibility without choice is not responsibility—it's a burden, fault, or blame. But if someone takes responsibility for being source in an organization, then everyone else has the SPACE to be responsible—they have a choice about being responsible—and true responsibility can then exist.

The only kind of responsibility most people know is responsibility by agreement. When you and I get together and make HIM responsible, that's not responsibility. That's burden. That's blame. That's fault. That's guilt. Or that's authority. That's totally different from responsibility. Responsibility begins with the willingness to be cause in the matter.

What I wanted to do was create an organization in which each person could be 100 percent responsible for everything without regard to anybody else's degree of responsibility—an organization in which people had the opportunity to discover the source of things—what created them or caused them—instead of giving explanations or mere justification for what happened . . .

As the organization developed, I discovered a few other elements you have to put into an organization or institution—not to make it work, but to discover what you need to know in order to make it work. The next one I discovered was COMMUNICATIONS. So I developed the Communication Workshop, which at the time was primarily for the est staff. After taking that workshop, the people in the organization began to communicate with each other, and guess what we found out! We found out that nobody communicates. There was an incredible mass of talk and words (symbols) and forms and no communication—which is obviously what you would discover if you began really to communicate. When you find out what communication really is, the first thing you discover is that you don't have any.

The next element I discovered that you need to make an organization work is RELATIONSHIP. As it became clear that the self at the level of relationship was transformed— which I realized in the training that you all created the space for me to go through—I saw that I had to create space for relationship to exist in the organization.

And that's what the Making Relationship Work course came out of. Staff members had to have the space in which to question each other and doubt each other and get angry at each other and have upsets with each other. The space had to be created for that to happen, for it to be OKAY for that to happen. Staff members needed to have a safe space in which to communicate, and they had to know that they already were related for all that to happen. So, a third element that had to be present in the organization was relationship.

Fourth and finally, in order to discover what made an organization work I needed to create the space for INTEGRITY—a willingness to reveal and acknowledge the truth.

Source, communication, relationship, integrity—those were the qualities I found had to be in an organization in order to be able to discover what is required to make an organization work.[3]

As I began to appreciate the different levels of transformation—individuality, relationship, institution and society, there seemed to be a pattern in the demonstration of each of the last four ages of the Zodiac. Remember, consciousness is not a process of seeing the truth as much as it is a process of seeing what is not the truth. The last three ages were demonstrations for this age of what is not the truth about each level of transformation.

The age of Taurus, the Bull, which covers approximately 6,000 to 4,000 B.C. includes both the story of the Garden of Eden and the great flood. We have already discussed the significance of the fall from the Tree of Life to the Tree of Knowledge. Noah represents the ending of the old world where he was effect and the opportunity to begin a new world as source. The world of the many pearls was to be given up for the one pearl-of-great-price.

Most people assume that if we could just get rid of all the bad people, the world would become a paradise. We think the same about ourselves. If we could just get rid of all the vain, greedy, foolish parts and keep the obedient, faithful and loving part, we would be "perfect." The story of Noah, fact or myth, demonstrates that even when we do so, the "one" soon becomes many and the age ends with the Tower of Babel. The Bull is a loner. He will not stand for any competition and claims dominion over the herd. The self, as the double mind, can repent, improve, or do anything it pleases to make the mind single, and the more it changes the more it stays the same. The Age of Taurus was a demonstration that transformation is not produced by eliminating all the competition of non-agreement.

The Age of Aries, the Ram, which covered the period of 2,000 B.C. to the time of Christ includes the story of Abraham, Isaac and Jacob, along with his twelve sons and the story of Moses leading the descendents of Jacob out of Egypt to the promised land.

People think that if we could just get our loved ones around us, work for and serve each other in the family, we would be transformed. We would be free of selfishness and pettiness because we would be kith and kin. In other words, we would be transformed by the strength of the family relationship. Abraham demonstrated the ultimate love of God by being willing to sacrifice his only son in obedience. Notice that the boy's life was spared by an alternate sacrifice—the ram caught in the thicket. The ram, a male sheep, symbolizes the flock or family. Abraham was to rear up a great and holy family, and through it, save society. But it didn't work. Within three generations they were slaves in Egypt. So they were given a perfect ram, Moses, who got them free by putting lamb's blood on their door posts. They were freed by the miraculous destruction of Egypt and the dividing of the sea, fed by manna from heaven, taught by a total law of good and evil, judged by holy men of equity, and blessed by a land flowing with milk and honey. And they failed. Their sad demonstration was culminated and fulfilled by the sacrifice of the Lamb of God, the infant ram.

During the last 2,000 years since Christ, we have seen the demonstration of the Age of Pisces, the Fish. It is highlighted by the birth, death and resurrection of Christ and the ministry of the twelve apostles who established the "perfect" institution, the Kingdom of God, known as the Church of Christ.

As each of us discovers that, first, we cannot seem to be perfect in and of ourselves alone, and, second, that we are not able to be perfect even with the united relationship of our family, then our only hope appears that we must become a perfect part of a perfect whole. Only through a perfect institution, it seemed, could we perfect the earth. But the church did not work either.

The net caught the fish, but the fish ate the net. The Dark Ages of Western Civilization were presided over by the church. Practically all the breakthroughs in culture, economics, science, literature and art were opposed by the great institutions of "liberation and enlightenment." At the ending of this last age, we have had two massive world wars of Christians fighting Christians and a world dangerously divided by two opposing concepts of liberty—Freedom-To versus Freedom-From. Our age has culminated in the massive conversion to the concept of the ultimate institution, which is not the family nor the church, but the STATE. Everything from the welfare state to the communist state has been "believed in" as the solution for misery, greed and insecurity.

Although each age has provided great strides in conquering the natural world, there has been no conquest of the natural man. To summarize, we could list the last three ages as follows:

Age of the Bull: Failure on the level of individuality. Noah and the attempt to make a holy (perfect) world.

Age of the Ram: Failure on the level of relationship–family. Israel and the attempt to establish a holy (perfect) family.

Age of the Fish: Failure on the level of institution. Twelve Apostles and the attempt to build a holy (perfect) church.

So for six thousand years, mankind has been striving, trying, struggling and progressing—yet never BEING. Every approach to the knowledge of good and evil falls short. Completeness cannot be found in the "one," the "group" or the "order." Transformation does not come from ideal circumstances and conditions. It comes from turning away from what the self thinks it is and is not. That would be the Age of Aquarius, the Gardener, the man who carries his own water.

---

1. Graduate Review, Nov. 1976, p. 4
2. Graduate Review, Nov. 1976, p. 4
3. Graduate Review, Nov. 1976, pp. 4-5

CHAPTER 14

Confronting the Evil in est

In 1976, when Werner Erhard spoke to 20,000 est graduates about the transformation of est, he had a great deal to say about how the institution of est had become a "principality" without him even knowing it. In this chapter we will let him tell his own story of how this could happen when he had known in advance the possible traps and pitfalls.

> When you create an organization you create both the good and the evil inherent in organization. The question is whether you can come to take responsibility for the evil, to own it, to complete it and therefore to master it—or whether you become the effect of it, either by hiding it, resisting it, or being the victim of it.
>
> I want to be clear with you about what the word "evil" means. Evil is selling or trading aliveness for survival. When you give up your aliveness to dominate, when you give up your wholeness or completion in order to justify yourself— that's what evil is.
>
> I caution you about getting into an "us versus them" thing. I could be talking about any institution. I could be talking about the government or the welfare system. I could be talking about the church, about medicine, about the place where you work, about the clubs you belong to. It's all the same stuff. Here, I'm talking about the institution called the est organization because that's the one I've got available to me and that's the one I used in the training that created an opportunity for transformation for the self at the level of organization . . .

Werner uses the word "training" in a specific sense. The dictionary says training is "instruction coupled with practice in the use of one's own powers." The self, being Total Source, is suppressed in

136

our lives because of our confined stupor of limitation, illusion and distortion. Training, in the est sense, is almost like rehabilitation, enabling the self to disidentify from the mind, to practice using the power of "self-remembering," getting in touch with the direct experience of self.

The formal training of my self at the level of organization really began about six months before Stewart Emery left, while Stewart was in the process of leaving and Don Cox was taking over and managing and organizing the organization. That's where I placed it in time. Now that it's happened, in retrospect one can see that it was always going on.

Stewart Emery was the first person Werner trained as a trainer. He left in 1975.

What happened at about the time of Stewart's leaving is that the evil that any institution or organization is began to crystallize . . . When Stewart Emery left est, I (myself, the self at the level of individuality and the self at the level of relationship) had no problem with that. My relationship with Stewart is complete.

Yet that Stewart thought he had to leave est revealed some evil, crystallized some evil, at the level of organization. The evil was there. Nobody put it there. Stewart's leaving just crystallized it, and I was able to avoid seeing the evil that was crystallizing because I just stopped being the organization. I moved over to relationship and experienced the evil in that context. As relationship there was no threat; it was all complete. But, as organization, I simply wasn't confronting it.

The next thing that happened was that other staff members began to leave. Many who didn't leave were thinking about leaving. Not only were many graduates making the est organization wrong, many staff members also were making it wrong—complaining about it, griping about it, being at the effect of it.

There were staff members—people with whom I had an absolutely complete relationship, people to whom I would give my life without worrying a bit, people I would trust with anything—who did the most incredibly treacherous things that you could imagine. For example, people who had been given the privilege of intimacy violated that privilege. Some former staff members said things in public (in a different context) that were said to them in the context of a relationship (family), and also misrepresented intimate conversions.

Some staff members used relationships with graduates, who supported them because they served people as est staff members, for their own personal ends.

As this was going on, we also lost sight of our purpose and did some things for our convenience rather than to serve the purpose of est. We became increasingly concerned with the survival of the organization.

Throughout all this, I avoided a threat to my self at the level of organization, because I didn't confront it as organization. I confronted it as individuality and relationship. I didn't feel betrayed by the treachery; I didn't feel that the person was bad. Our relationship was complete. In the space of our relationship nothing they could do would be "bad."

Now, I just want you to get that the evil had been crystallizing and you and I had been able to avoid confronting it by shifting from experiencing it as organization to experiencing it as relationship or individuality. I dealt with it as I dealt with the inaccuracies and misrepresentations in the media. I never had to retaliate or fight back. I never had to justify or explain them to you as there is no survival in my relationship with you. That doesn't mean I don't want to communicate. I just never felt the need to explain those things because I was quite clear that your relationship was complete. I think, however, that a lot of people's *minds* thought that my not responding to that stuff was an affirmation of it.

See, I'm very clear about lies. Lies persist, and the truth doesn't. And the stuff that persists holds no sway in the universe. I am totally willing to stay with the truth, that doesn't persist and does hold sway. Besides which, if you don't react to lies, if you don't resist them, that provides the opportunity to take responsibility for them and to complete them. Lies merely persist. The truth is eternal, so it all turns out.

The media made an important contribution to this training that I've been through. Every time something in the media expressed doubts and fears, it gave agreement to your doubts, your fears, your lack of trust. And every time any of you submerged your experience by being quiet (by being a "closet graduate"), or explaining away and justifying your participation (to prove you hadn't been conned), that allowed the evil to reveal itself, that was the evil crystallizing.

During this time I had thought that the biggest fear that people had was the fear of being conned. Recently, in a conversation with a graduate, I realized that the fear of being conned is not what really runs people. What really runs people, where people's behavior comes from, is the fear that someone else will *think* they have been conned. If you don't get anything out of this evening but an understanding of that mechanism and how evil it is, that would make it worth your time.

IT'S IMPORTANT TO GET THIS. Every time you didn't share your experience of transformation and every time you denied that experience (by saying "I got something from the training, but . . .") you substituted survival for aliveness and satisfaction. The source of that behavior and those comments (when and to the extent it occurred) was your need to prove to others that *you* didn't get brainwashed, *you* didn't believe it, *you* weren't proselytizing—in short that *you* weren't conned.

So it's not enough for you to *know* that you weren't conned. If anybody *thinks* you were conned, some of you go into the closet. Into a defensive posture. Into a proving posture.

What I had been doing (at the level of organization), then, was resisting people's thinking that I had conned anybody. As organization I didn't like anybody thinking I had.

So it was all crystallizing. You were out there mumbling and grumbling: "The training is terrific, but the organization stinks." Remember? That's another way of avoiding responsibility for the evil.

It took everybody, by the way, each of those individual 80,000 positions, to produce this training of the self as organization. All of you made an important contribution: the ones who made est wrong, the ones who took responsibility for their experience and shared and communicated it. Everyone was necessary to the transformation of self at the level of organization. I'm not talking about someone else; I'm talking about *you*. Every one of you was necessary.

Last year, before all this stuff had crystallized noticeably, we had planned two seminars for graduates in the media, one in Los Angeles for February, 1976, and the other in New York for March. February arrived and the Los Angeles seminar was beautiful. But a few days before the media seminar in New York, an article in *New Times* magazine came out which was kind of like the last straw in the crystallization of the evil. It further validated and solidified the doubts and fears and suspicions.

I was in New York, in my room at the Plaza Hotel just before the New York Media Seminar, with all this evil crystallizing and reports about how we've had to cut down the expense base, and how important staff members have left, and how the graduates are grumbling, and all the media stuff is providing the graduates with agreement, and so on.

To top it all off, Morty Lefkoe, Manager of the est Public Information Office, came to see me and said, "Werner, I'm in trouble. The articles are even starting to get to me. It's not that I believe the specific accusations, because I'm on the inside and I know the facts. But I have had some doubts and fears about you and est, and these articles are providing my mind with so much agreement that I can't ignore my doubts and fears any longer. They have become more real for me than my experience."

If that's where Morty was, you can imagine where other graduates probably would have had to be. They didn't even have the direct contact with the facts. Somewhere along the line, it had to appear that maybe it really was all a con. Whatever value you got from it, it looked as if you had to hold onto and hide and not let anybody see, because if you *acknowledge* the value and then it's labeled a con, you're stuck—you've been conned, you've been found out, your worst fears have been realized.

Obviously, I had to take responsibility for that. I'm the guy who invented responsibility, right? So I had no choice but to take responsibility for it. So I wasn't really being responsible.

I knew I could not go into the New York media event that way. That would have been chopping a hole in the bottom of the boat. I had to get centered.

At that point, just as things were coming to a head, I got a call from Harry Margolis. Harry is est's attorney, and he thinks that his value to est is being the devil's advocate. Harry questions everything, he belittles everything, he complains about everything, nothing is all right, everything stinks, no matter what we do it's wrong. So here I am in the midst of this incredible pile of evil, trying to get centered, and now the devil's advocate is on the phone to tell me how bad it all is. Terrific!

Now there's one other aspect to all this that you need to see before I tell you about Harry's call. I want you to get that I created est as something to serve people, and here it was crystallizing as evil.

If the whole thing were just evil, you'd just say to hell with it and leave it. That's no dilemma, that's no problem. There's no frustration if it's just evil. It was the exact opposite of that. You see, I knew where this whole thing came from. I was there when we put it together. I know the sincerity and the intention and the willingness to give up personal concerns on the part of the people who created this organization. I know what people put into the est organization. I know this organization.

This organization has created the space for transformation for thousands and thousands of people. The value produced has been incredible. People's lives have started working; their jobs have become nurturing. In addition to that, thousands and thousands of graduates had put themselves on the line. People with careers that they'd built painstakingly over the years were willing to stand in the midst of their careers and acknowledge the value that they'd gotten from participating in the training. These were people who were putting out their absolute best.

And there were the staff members who had literally given up careers, and/or their selfish, small interests, to serve people. To make the world work. These people were willing to continually get off it, and get off it, and get off it.

That's what was at stake. All of *that* was apparently culminating in this evil. If it had been evil that had culminated in evil there would have been no problem. But it was the absolute best I had ever seen in the universe, the best that I could imagine, that was crystallizing into evil. It was not the worst of people, it was the best of people. Can you get the kind of hopelessness and frustration of that? Can you make that real for yourself? And it was at the height of that feeling that the devil's advocate called.

Now in fact, Harry's value to me and to est has not been as a devil's advocate. His real value is his integrity. Harry Margolis is one of those very important people in my life, because of those times that he has created space for me to see it the way it is. There have been times when I have been tempted to give in to the pressure of public opinion. Harry has been the one person who always gave me the space to discover my self—to discover what the truth was in any given circumstance, so I never had to bow to or give in to public opinion. I could be true to the self.

And that's what happened in this phone call. Harry said: "I am clear that est is capable of making a unique contribution in the world. And you've got some important decisions to make. est is at a major crossroad.

"One road is to close est down, to give the training to those people who have already enrolled and finish off the seminars that have started and pay off the staff. If you did that, you would always be considered an honorable man. You'd get out looking good.

"Werner, I have been around you. I also know that you are clever enough to overcome the problem and make est succeed." (He meant succed in the world of agreement.) "If you do that, what you yourself have created will be buried in the success."

(At that point I realized that what happens to organizations is that they become successful and what that means is that they hide the evil that they are. In institutions, success hides the evil that exists in them.)

Harry then said that there was one other option. He said, and these are his exact words, "You've got to give up being a *little* son of a bitch."

And Harry underlined the world "little." What he meant was that I would have to be big enough to take responsibility for the evil of the organization. I would have to create true responsibility—not accept it at effect.

Harry was right about the possibilities. It's just possible that I could have been clever enough and stupid enough to overcome the evil. Somehow the space that I got out of that communication with Harry allowed me to be clear, and what I got clear about is so obvious by now that telling you is anti-climactic. What I got clear about is that I had been "on it"—that as organization I had lost my self (to be more technically accurate, I had identified my self at the level of organization as my mind) and that that made survival the purpose of the organization. The way I had it wired up, the survival of my self as organization was being threatened.

It's easy to see your self as individuality. Not so hard to see your self as relationship. But to get you (or me) as institution, that's tough. And that's what I'd like you to get. I had begun to protect my own survival. Not my own personal survival, that was not an issue. And not my survival as relationship. What I hadn't seen was that me-as-organization was a pure survival game.

I'd like you to see that that's true for you, too. I'd like you to see that you back off being institution (and the est organization) when your survival is threatened.

If I were to give you all the details of this particular training I've been describing, you would see that it is absolutely parallel to the est training. Right after Harry's phone call, it was as if I was in the middle of the Anatomy of the Mind part of the training—you know, when you find out that, "Oh, my God, I've spent my whole life trying to survive and what I am is a survival machine." And remember when you get through the heaviness and the horribleness of it, and you burst into laughter and say, "So what?"

Well, that's where I was. I said to myself somewhat sarcastically: "Wait a minute. They're going to take the organization away from me? So what? I'll have no alternative but to give up working 20 hours a day and go sailing? So what? You mean I'll have to give up having people question my motives and question my sincerity? You mean I'll have to give up being misrepresented? You mean I'll have to give up being responsible for training a whole staff of people and developing dozens of programs and never having a spare minute? You mean I'll have to give it all up and just have a love affair with the 80,000 people I've trained: You've got to be kidding!"

Well, you know how people burst out laughing in the training when they get it? That's where I was for two days. I walked into the New York media seminar and all those media graduates—those caged tigers who'd been poked with the *New Times* article for a couple of days—they all spontaneously stood up and applauded. That acknowledgment just came right out of our relationship. And it was all complete for them at the level of relationship. The caged animal part was about themselves as organization, not as relationship. They had stood up to acknowledge their experience of a complete relationship. They were incredible.

But then the event began and we began to get into the organization, and it was completely different. For example, there was this very distinguished editor who stood up and screamed: "Look, if you'd only admit you're in it for the money, then it would be all right!"

And at some point I began to let them go through it and I would say, "Even if that were true, so what? What's the point?"

And they quoted from the articles to prove that est was evil. And I said: "So est is evil, what's the point?" "Yeah, I got that, now what?" "So what?"

At that point I felt what people who know they got it feel right after the Anatomy of the Mind in the training, when some asshole stands up and asks another question or defends his position. It's a mixture of disbelief and amusement. It's sort of like: "C'mon now. You must be kidding!"

It was a great night. For the next two days in New York, it all began to fall out. It all began to get clear, and I confronted every bit of the evil, piece by piece. I could be responsible for the evil—at cause rather than at effect. I was clear that I had created every bit of the evil. I now experienced being 100% responsible for all of the evil in the est organization.

Suddenly, instead of not being able to avoid being responsible for the inaccuracies and misrepresentations in the media, I could be totally responsible for them. In fact, they were incredibly useful, because what they did was to crystallize and reveal and allow people to confront their own doubt.

This is more than a story, it is a demonstration. It is said that the hidden teachings are not so much taught as they are demonstrated. Words are only concepts. Seeing is insight. Werner, in his total willingness to reveal the truth, has created the SPACE for many of us to stop being "on it" and get "off it." In all my years of working in organizations—business, church, political, educational and even family—I have never come closer or got clearer in seeing what goes wrong and what is necessary for an organization to work.

Even more incredible for me is that Werner's experience of transformation on the level of organization has given me a greatly expanded understanding of the atonement of Christ. We will take that up in the next chapter.

---

1. Graduate Review, Nov. 1976

CHAPTER 15

The Atonement of Jesus Christ

We are all aware of the way the atonement of the Savior is understood and appreciated by most Christians. The ordeal at Gethsemane, the trial, public execution and his death are all seen as a heartbreaking tragedy required by our massive sins. Only the triumphant resurrection puts a silver lining on the dismal cloud of sorrow.

Something very different begins to happen when one sees beyond the illusion of our being separate entities. It was not the Father sending his Son off to be the scapegoat, it was not the ultimate example of service and sacrifice. Self was on that cross. The Father was on the cross. You and I were on that cross. It was self as Self being 100% responsible for EVERYTHING. And that can smart a lot. That can really hurt. It was Self as a conscious human being, a mortal person who knew he was the Source of IT ALL, who took all the incompletions, all the blaming, all the irresponsibility, all the vengeance, all the hatred and all the anti-agape. It was not anything he wanted to do, nor anything that he had to do. It was something that he was totally WILLING TO DO.

Of course, we all know what the judgmental double mind wants to happen. It doesn't want Christ on the cross. It wants all the guilty ones up there instead. What about Adam? He should have been nailed up there. Well, who do you think was on that cross? It was Adam. In fact Christ is called the LAST ADAM. Yes, and Cain, Pharaoh, Saul, Hitler, Dillinger, and everyone else—even you and me. Self was on the cross. That would also include Enoch, Melchisedec, Moses, Abraham, Mary, Peter, George Washington, Lincoln and everyone else—even you and me. The Word was on the cross, and the word was with God and the word was God. As Paul declares, "For by him (Jesus) were all things created that are in heaven and that are in earth, visible and invisible, whether they be thrones or dominions or principalities or powers, all things were created BY HIM AND FOR HIM. And he is before all things and by him ALL THINGS CONSIST . . .for it pleased the Father that in him (consciously) should ALL FULNESS DWELL."[1]

In the last chapter Werner described an atonement of himself for est. Atonement means at-one-ment, putting it all back together in one. est had become fragmented. In its struggle for survival and success, it had developed a life of its own. It had become more than a means, it had become the end. A total sacrifice of all those in it was not even going to be enough. est was becoming, not being. It was incomplete. Werner was trying very hard to correctly serve the institution of est by being responsible. Then, thanks to a phone call from the devil's advocate, he woke up and went to the cross.

Werner saw that he, and he alone, had done it all. In the words of Paul, we might say that he had created all the things in est, visible and invisible, whether they be thrones or dominions or principalities or powers, all things were created by him and for him. And it was truly terrible and it was truly wonderful and besides that, it was okay. est was not important and est was very valuable. It was okay for est not to be and it was okay for est to be. In fact, that is what est means in Latin: IT IS.

As soon as Werner experienced that est did not have to survive and therefore no one had to fix it, he was free to make at-one-ment, which means to let est be back on purpose. est ceased to be a principality and again became a tool, the word, self on the level of institution. In that moment, the old est died and a few days later, a new est was resurrected.

Werner has made it clear that since he is totally responsible for everything in est, no one else has to be. Since they do not have to be, they can really be responsible. He has invited you and me to choose to be the organization of est, if we would like. To experience the institution as being the total creator of it—just exactly the way it is today, with all the staff and assistants, the programs and procedures, the upsets and frailties and all the rest. It is not "me" versus "it" or "them." It is "I" as self playing the game of est, including Werner, the advisory board, the staff, the offices, etc. Being responsible, we can act responsibly. That means that when I see something which is not working well or might work better, I may decide to talk to someone who can do something about it and not to someone who can't do anything about it except give me agreement. Everything I experience in est is from the source of self. And do you know what? It is not half bad. In fact it is pretty good! I can see that I have even created the place in est where I fit in, and that's not half bad either.

If one can really experience being est, which is not that difficult to do, then one can look at the infinite and universal atonement of the Savior. He took all the responsibility so we do not have to take ANY. Therefore we are free to be 100% responsible for

EVERYTHING. We are source. And do you know what? It's not half bad! In fact, it all is downright terrific. What is IS INCREDIBLE. What is IS MIRACULOUS, AWESOME, MINDBOGGL-ING.

In this way we may be washed clean and pure by the blood, the life flow, of Christ. We may be cleansed from all sin, meaning all the missing of the point. Our eye may be single and filled with light, having no darkness. There can be no basis for blame, jealousy, anger, judgment, greed or competition, yet there is also space for these as well. Thus, there would be no fear.

> And we have known and believed the love that God hath to us. God is love and he that dwelleth in love DWELLETH (experiences life) IN GOD AND GOD IN HIM. . .
> Herein is our love made PERFECT, that we may have boldness in the day of judgment (day of accountability), BECAUSE AS HE IS, SO ARE WE IN THIS WORLD. . .
> There is no fear in love; but perfect love casteth out fear because fear hath torment. He that feareth is not made perfect in love.[2]

Agape, perfect love, is understanding who we are, that we are self, the SOURCE OF ALL EFFECT.

---

1. Col. 1:16 & 19
2. I John 4:17-18

CHAPTER 16
The Transformation of est

In this chapter we will give the concluding portion of Werner's talk on The Transformation of est. One of the most significant notions he will discuss is that organizations succeed out of agreement, and the need for agreement is also the reason they do not work—why they sacrifice purpose and aliveness for success and survival. This is not to say agreement is wrong. It is only the *need* for agreement which destroys aliveness. In the religious sense, agreement is usually what people mean by conversion. Conversion has a meaning in the hidden teachings of being totally turned about. This is what is necessary for an organization to be transformed so that it will work.

Werner calls this quality alignment. As he says below, "Agreement is where everybody is GOING TO the same place; alignment is where everybody is COMING FROM the same place." In the previous chapter, this was described as atonement—at-one-ment. It is coming from the same SOURCE.

In the two days following that New York media event (which was on a Friday), I just kept confronting more of the evil and taking responsibility for it, not moving back into relationship where it was all already handled.

That Sunday the training that I've been talking about was completed. It happened at about 11 o'clock at night as I watched the David Susskind show. David's show that night was going to be an argument about the validity of est—pro and con, conflict.

What happened was that David had asked the New York est Center to invite some gradutes to be in the audience. The graduates were there, and some of the people on the panel who were going to argue about est were late. Sandy Baron, an est graduate who is in the entertainment business, was in the audience and said to David, "Look, you could put together a great show by interviewing the graduates here."

And David said, "Well, we'll try it."

He did try it and, to his credit, he had the courage to air it.

It was the most incredible thing I've ever seen on television in my life. There were about 40 graduates there, and at no time during the entire two hours did I ever see any graduate ever make anybody or anything wrong. Not once. Not even a little one slipped in underneath. I was so moved I can't tell you.

David is a real pro. Here were 40 people under skillful attack from a guy playing devil's advocate in order to create a controversial show. David would twist around what they said and they wouldn't even correct him. What they did was to continue to come from their experience for two hours. Two whole hours! And they didn't even have to agree with each other.

I want you to get the power that that represents, not to have to use somebody else's stuff to make your own stuff real. Nobody felt called on to give the benefit of his or her infinite wisdom or to evaluate or agree with what someone else said. When David asked a question, they simply looked inside their experience for something that related to the question and shared the experience. And if he took the answer and played devil's advocate and twisted it around, and said, "What about that?" to the next person, they did not say, "Well, no, you're wrong." They didn't even imply that he was wrong. It was a beautiful two hours. That really completed the training for me.

At that point, I realized that the est organization was complete. I don't have to worry about its survival, just as I don't have to worry about my survival. My self is absolute.

My self as individuality was not born, is not going to die, always was, always will be, is the space in which time occurs, is the space in which distance and position occur, and is the space in which all form occurs.

My self as relationship is also complete. You can't threaten my survival as relationship. My relationship with you is complete. You can hate me; it's all right. It's just your way of completing the barriers to our relationship which is already complete. There is no threat. It's complete. Do you get it?

And as organization my self (the self) is also complete. As I said earlier about transformation: the self is complete and *is being complete*. What I realized Sunday night is that the est organization *is* complete (completely created) and is *being complete* (completely started). Its survival is not at issue. est just is. Those 40 people had demonstrated to me that there's no way to kill it. If we never did another training, est would go on. The est organization as a game of survival is over, for the self. The self has become itself at the level of organization. That's completion.

Maybe it won't be called est. So what's the difference what we call it? When I started it, it wasn't about calling it est. Maybe we won't ever have any more trainings. So what? Never mind what name you want to call it, never mind what form it's got—the self manifesting itself as institution *is*. That's it. Nobody *has* to be responsible for making est work. Nobody has to be responsible for its survival because it can't not survive. The self evidencing itself as institution *is*. That's what I got clear about on Sunday night and that's when the training was over.

Remember when you got home after the training and just had to share your experience with whoever was there? Well, later that evening after the Susskind Show, about dawn actually, I wrote a paper, and this paper is my sharing. It is not necessarily est policy or an actual program that I am announcing, but a concrete manifestation of the experience I was having. While the paper is about the creation of a guest program for est, what it is really about is the space from which I intend all est activities to come.

First, I want to show you something. Survival of the self at the level of *individuality* evidences itself by being right/ making others wrong, dominating/avoiding domination, self-justification/invalidation of others—self righteousness. Survival of the self at the level of *relationship* evidences itself as entanglements and involvement.

What about survival of self at the level of *organization*? When an organization is its mind instead of its self, how does that mind evidence its survival? Effort! Struggle! Red tape. Complexity. Work that produces no satisfaction for anyone, just upset and annoyance. So the self as organization evidences survival, not by playing right/wrong, nor by entanglement and involvement, but by effort.

So the first point of the paper I wrote on the guest program has to do with taking the effort, the struggle out of est.

1. The first fundamental of the guest program is that we will schedule trainings on the basis of—

   a. demand (interest) from graduates for trainings to facilitate their interest in and intention to share the training with others, *and*

   b. demand (interest) from guests for training to facilitate their interest in and intention to participate in the training.

   We will reduce the number of trainings if necessary, raise the cost of training if necessary, become more able to communicate if necessary, cease doing the training altogether if necessary, or whatever is necessary to conduct the guest program so that it serves graduates *and* serves guests. We will not schedule trainings based on our need.

That doesn't mean we won't be putting the training out to people—simply that we will schedule a number of trainings consistent with your willingness and interest and your ability to share the experience you had in est. If that means doing one training a year, then we'll do that.

2. The second fundamental is to serve the graduates by providing a guest program based on supporting graduates' interest in:

   a. making a contribution to the aliveness of others, and

   b. enriching their own lives and expanding their experience of aliveness, satisfaction, and completion.

That's the purpose of the guest program—not for est to get people in the training, but to provide an opportunity for graduates to share their experience and to make a contribution to others, if that's what they want to do.

As I said before, you don't need to do anything, I will handle it all. My self at the level of organization is transformed. I don't need anybody any more. Honest, I will do it all myself. Just by myself I'll be an organization. No kidding. You created me—I'll do it for you. You aren't needed for est to survive. It would be terrific if everybody got that.

3. The third fundamental is to allow the graduates to participate in and be responsible for and play the game of *est, only on the basis of getting more out of it than they put into it*. Any graduate who chooses to participate in the guest program is responsible for getting at least as much as they give.

4. The fourth fundamental is that the guest program does not come out of comfort or reasonableness, but satisfaction, aliveness and completion. Also, not uncomfortableness or unreasonableness. Comfort or discomfort, reasonableness or unreasonableness are okay only when they come out of being appropriate to satisfaction or aliveness. It is a *requirement* that sharing guests be enlivening and satisfying.

5. The fifth fundamental is the heart of what I manifested concretely out of this training. It is that est is not a function of agreement or conformity. est does not come out of agreement or disagreement with something or someone. While est may be expressed or manifested or may exist in your mind, est does not come from the world or from anyone's mind.

We do not require agreement or the absence of disagreement to participate in est. Agreement and disagreement are a function of the mind, and while est manifests itself in the world of agreement and disagreement (the mind), these are not where est comes from.

est comes from the self itself. est comes from source. What source is, is the self itself. From source we have created a game called est. est is a space—a context—manifesting itself as a game, as a process, as something going on. est is "our" game. What creates space for you to particapte in est is alignment with source, rather than agreement with someone or something.

Organizations will never work as a function of agreement. Organizations *succeed* as function of agreement, and the agreements bury the evil. What makes organizations work is *alignment*. Not agreement. That's the breakthrough. Alignment is the self itself being with the self itself. What makes an organization work is the expression of the self itself. The self at the level of organization has to know that there is alignment and that agreement is unnecessary. You don't have to trap anyone into agreement. You don't even have to agree with the principles of est. All you have to do is experience alignment.

I no longer have to do anything to make the organization work. All I need to "do" is to experience alignment, and I do. When I experience alignment, I am transformed at the level of organization. I know that we are aligned. And I don't require you to agree in any way.

An organization that *works* transforms the quality of institutions. And it does so—it works—out of alignment. Agreement is where everybody is *going to* the same place; alignment is where everybody is *coming from* the same place.

I don't expect this to mean anything to you at this point, any more than when I tell people that what is, is and what isn't, isn't. That doesn't mean anything either. I am not trying to get you to understand something. I am not trying to inform you. My intention is to create the space for you to experience your self as institution.

est is our game and we wholeheartedly invite you to participate with us in playing our game. We welcome you and invite you to make it "our" game for you. Who is the "our"? "Our" is anyone who is aligned with the self itself. We welcome you and invite you to make it "our" game for yourself to whatever degree it serves you to participate and contribute—not because *you have to* or because *we need you*. To the degree that "our" needs you, it isn't "our."

The name of the game in est is service.

We invite you to create, cause, contribute to and play in est to the degree that it serves you to do so. The agreement is that you are responsible for being served at least as much as you serve.

We also create the space for you not to play. If what you want to do is to create our getting the job done with you going to the beach, that's okay, too. Your contribution to "our" is to go to the beach and create our getting the job done. You can count on us.

I do want to tell you that our organization—which includes you, by the way—has truly been courageous. It has had the courage to discover and take responsibility for its own unwillingness to acknowledge source and to be responsible for its own absence of relationship. It has had courage and the clarity and the guts and the bigness and the humanity to confront and take responsibility for its own absence of communication. And there was enough integrity in the organization for members of the staff to confront the absence of integrity and to take responsibility for it, for the treachery, for the evil that existed in the est organization.[1]

Werner has an aim for providing the training for forty million people around the world. Then he would like to see est as an organization come to an end. It may happen before then or after, that is not the point. What really interests me is that est is not designed to go on forever. It is a tool that can be used until other tools come along which can take over from there.

My experience with the est organization has been fairly limited and came after its transformation. From my own experience, it appears to me that the newborn baby is doing very well. Precision, clockwork, spontaneity, order, responsibility, fun, busy, expansive and careful are some of the words that come to mind when watching est work—and it does work.

1. Graduate Review, Nov. 1976

CHAPTER 17
The Transformation of the Church

It is with particular delight that I come to the subject of this chapter. We have already quoted Paul's description of the work of the church—"for the perfecting of the saints . . . unto the measure of the stature of the fulness of Christ." Peter was no less positive: "According as his divine power hath given unto us ALL THINGS that pertain unto LIFE AND GODLINESS . . . that by these ye might be partakers of the DIVINE NATURE, having escaped the corruption that is in the world through lust."[1]

John adds his description as being that of fellowship. The Greek word we translate as fellowhip is koinonia, which means to "communicate in communion." It is a getting in touch, the direct experience of the self, being the same self. John says, "That ye also may have fellowship with us and truly our fellowship is with the Father and with his Son Jesus Christ . . . If we say that we have fellowship with him and walk in darkness, we lie and do not the truth. But if we walk in the light AS HE IS IN THE LIGHT, we have fellowship one with another, and the blood of Jesus Christ his Sön cleanseth us FROM ALL SIN."[2]

There is no need to look back over these last nineteen centuries to see how much and how little of these rich treasures have been harvested. It is here and now that the kingdom is at hand. The Christian churches do not stand with empty hands. They are made up of some of the greatest people on earth. Much of the clergy is bright, experienced and marvelously trained. Handsome and appropriate facilities

are abundantly spread across the land. The churches
have the organizations, the dedication and the means.
This is true of Catholic, Protestant and independent
churches alike. And let us not leave out the Jewish
synagogues. They have also been working on this
very dream for a long time. In fact, quite a book
could be written entitled "Judaism and est." Look for
yourself in chapter thirty of the Book of
Deuteronomy.

The task at hand is to get UNSTUCK. The
churches and congregations of today are stuck in the
survival-by-being-right game. There is a massive
crystallization of evil in churches. A new minister,
just out of seminary, who faces it for the first time
finds it very hard to believe. Pettiness, selfishness,
bigotry, politics, hair splitting and even hair pulling
are all just below the well-scrubbed surface of the
Sunday morning congregation. There is little perfecting of the saints, more perfecting of our
positionalities, our stories, our points of view. Remember, though this is evil, it is not bad. This evil is
actually perfect because it is a direct message to us of
where we are at. It may be the ball moving away from
the hand, yet it is all part of the great transformation
of the church which is coming to pass. We may be
approaching the point where we stop moving away
from Christ, hold still in mid air, and then start
returning to the Hand of Being.

It has been my own experience that est may provide a key to the transformation of the churches. It is
a way to open wide the doors of our well furnished
sanctuaries. It appears inevitable. Sooner or later we
are going to have more and more ministers, priests
and rabbis become est graduates. Those who have

already taken the training are being transformed in their church work. One of these days a group of church leaders is going to ask Werner to assist them in developing a special est Christian Training and follow-up courses by skilled trainers who can get the job done. Of course a special Christianized standard training is not necessary AND it would also be a very good thing. For example, if a major denomination had a dozen trainers to put on trainings around the country for its members and any of their friends who wanted to come—and pay the price—that denomination would truly COME ALIVE. As the personal experience of transformation would work deeper and deeper into the lives of the people, ALIVENESS would inspire and complete a transformation of the congregation.

Why a special Christianized training? Because it would be fun to have, for one thing. Instead of people being called "assholes," they would get to be dumb "Scribes, Pharisees and hypocrites." That is exactly what most of us Christians are, you know. The training could be directly aimed at our big, false Christian ACT. We could be challenged to get off that Tree of Knowledge of Good and Evil that we have totally worshipped in lieu of the Tree of Life. We could be challenged for our false obedience and doubting faith. Just as the training does not make being an asshole bad, neither would being a hypocrite be bad. It just doesn't allow one's life to work, that is all.

The main advantage of a special Christianized est training is that "getting off it" would allow us to "get on with it" within the momentum of the existing organizations. Of course, this would be like putting new wine into old bottles and all be lost unless the

program came from the people of leadership in the
organization who had experienced, personally, transformation on the level of institution, being 100%
responsible as source. Many congregations are independent enough that this process of transformation
could be "sourced" by the local minister. In any
event, it looks to me like it is only a matter of time.
The hidden teachings have been hidden long enough.
It is time that all Christians accept the responsibility for their own transformation. Then, with a transforming Christianity, we are going to see a transformation of our Western society, including government,
business, unions, family and education. There will be
more:

> Assisting, less helping,
> Sharing, less preaching,
> Acknowledging, less judging,
> Choosing, less losing,
> Accepting, less competing,
> Winning, less beating,
> Alignment, less agreement,
> At-one-ment, less us-them-ment.
> Agape, less fear.

Already we have seen what some est graduates
have done in education, prisons, family and business.
When congregations experience transformation on the
level of individuality, the old barriers of fear will be
replaced by total acceptance. Praying will become
communication. Faith will become love. As transformation is experienced on the level of relationship,
projects will move toward transforming the families,
the worship services, the singing, the finances, the
participation. As transformation is experienced on the

level of organization, people will individually become totally responsible for the church. It will be Self, Christ, as institution, just the way the early apostles always knew it would some day be.

As the church gets back on purpose, it will cease to hide the evil. It will have the space for people to be real and reveal the truth with each other and to each other. People will be enjoyed and accepted for what they are and what they are not. The church will experience being viable in the world like it has never been before. There will be no more begging for the tithes of the people, no more passing of the plate. As the congregation takes responsibility for cooperative ventures, so also will they provide the financial support. People who choose to participate in church projects will find their lives being nurtured and fulfilled far more than the time and effort expended. No one will need Brownie Points.

As the church grows in true strength of cohesive action, there will be seen ever increasing horizons of opportunities. The problems of the community will be taken on in the neighborhood. Ways will be found to give everyone the chance to be self-sufficient and off the dole. The community will be tended like a garden, ending pollution and neglect. And it will be fun. Everyone will be getting at least twice as much out of it as they put into it. The reasons is that each is SOURCE. Each is tending his marvelous creation of the WORLD. Each is Christ, at where he is, seeing without division, living without fear.

What Christ had to say in the Sermon on the Mount will come to have much deeper meaning. The "poor in spirit," the "meek," are those who are stripped of "knowledge," lacking in preconceived opinions, unwilling to give all kinds of advice. Being unstuck, like little children, "theirs is the kingdom of heaven"—love, joy and peace. Peacemakers do not make peace by subduing opposition but by total understanding, agape-love, going the extra mile. The merciful are not the do-gooders, they are those who assist others to discover who they are.

To resist evil is to fight darkness. Light never fights anything, it only fills space where there was an absence of light. When Jesus was talking about adultery, he spoke of the lust after a woman in the heart. Lust means to worship the need to have ideal feelings. Adultery, like morality, has much greater meaning than sexual behavior. Adultery means to adulterate, mix the impure with the pure. Jesus stressed that real adultery is in our hearts and minds, in worshipping false union for personal gratification.

"Woman," to all of us, male and female, is our source, since we all came from the womb of woman. When we lust for power to control, we are worshipping "false cause," wanting to be source by power rather than being. This "trading aliveness for being right" is adultery of the heart which is far more deadly than sexual lust, it is the blindness of blasphemey. To "lust after a woman in the heart" is the life style of the double mind, the mind of pride and vanity.

When we experience who we are and that this vain way of seeing has been our "right eye," we will "pluck it out and cast it from" us. When we see that all our acts, coming from lust, are self-destructive rather than life-giving, though it be by our "right hand," we will "cut if off and cast it from" us.

What did Jesus mean when he said, "Whosoever shall put away his wife, except for fornication, causeth her to commit adultery, and whosoever shall marry her again committeth adultery"? When people take this statement as an unrevocable, eternal definition of good and evil, they get caught in inflexibility that can be worse than death. When we see that the subject is still fornication and adultery, we can see that "wife" may have a much deeper meaning than marriage partner. A wife is a helpmate. The true helpmate of self, whether male or female, is designed to be the mind. People are always trying to "put away" their nagging mind for a mind that is "more, better and different." Any attempt to change our mind, our helpmate, for any other reason than discovering the darkness of it—called its "fornication"—merely brings the mind to greater abuse (adultery) of its real function. We will also see that our "second handed minds" were taken from the unworkable beliefs and knowledge of others, thus bringing about the adulteration of the pure gift of life.

We have two sides of our carnal nature. One is vanity, the false image we create of ourselves, and the other is pride, the need to defend the false image. This is what makes us "two-faced." So when someone slaps one side of our face, one cheek, by hurting our vanity, we can turn the other cheek, and let him take our pride as well.

Taking "thought" means to worry and fret. As one experiences transformation on each of the three levels, thought about survival (which always has to do with tomorrow) ceases to be a matter of concern. Like Jesus marveled, we also see how Life does

clothe the grass of the field, the lilies in their glory
and the fowl of the air. It increasingly becomes remarkable to watch how life works out. Not that there
is total comfort. Not that there are no challenges to
meet—heaven forbid if there were none. But it becomes awesome to see how everything contributes to
greater ALIVENESS.

Then we see what it means to have taken the
Lord's name of God in vain, meaning with no purpose or value, when we keep saying I AM this or
that. Moses, before he received the commandment
"to not take the name of God in vain," was given the
name. It is "I AM."[3] The great revelation is to see
that "I Am" is what I am. All the rest that I identify
myself with is in VAIN. It is nothing. It is not
necessary.

There is no pride or vanity in being "I Am" for so
is everyone. This is BE-ING in oneness that enables
us to agape-love our enemies, those who despitefully
use us. Then we are PERFECT—complete, fulfilled,
on purpose—even as the total Infinite Being, the
Father is.

The Age of Aquarius is a couple of thousand years
long. We play a game to play, not to get it out of the
way. We are participants in this extraordinary time of
enlightenment. There is no way we can imagine the
world in the year 4,000 A.D. The year 2,000 A.D. is
enough to keep us well entertained. There are all
kinds of revolutions to witness, to resist or to assist.
The "frightening" problems of over-population,
energy shortage, pollution, crime, poverty, civil
rights, exploitation, armament race, education and
illness are only fruit of the FORBIDDEN TREE.
For example, I attended an all-day seminar that

Werner hosted and the smiling genius, Buckminster Fuller, conducted. He has made significant breakthroughs in a number of different disciplines of science. He informed us that he has demonstrated the workability of a program which could enable man on this earth to have *everyone* adequately housed, fed and clothed, using no fossil fuels, all within the next ten years. He said, "I am absolutely positive that we can do it but I am not at all optimistic that we will do it." So it will take us longer.

"Bucky" closed his fascinating lecture-demonstration by saying, "I'm not trying to counsel any of you to do anything really special except really to DARE TO THINK and to DARE TO GO WITH THE TRUTH; and to DARE TO REALLY LOVE COMPLETELY."[4]

Christianity and est! We are not talking about a marriage. We are talking about a revolution, a 180° conversion. Werner does not want est to become Christianity. Christianity does not need to become est. They are different and they are the same. They are doors to the Way, the Truth and the Life. Love is never in competition with love. Light is never in opposition to light.

As the Book of Revelation Testifies:

And the Spirit and the bride say, Come. And let him that heareth say, Come. And let him that is athirst come. And whosoever will, let him take of the Water of Life freely.[5]

---

1. II Peter 1:1-4
2. I John 1:3-7
3. Exodus 3:14
4. Graduate Review, December 1976, p. 4
5. Revelation 22:17

CHAPTER 18

Beyond The Beginning—
The Communication Workshop

The preceding seventeen chapters contain the book that I intended to write on Christianity and est. However, after it was finished, est provided an additional experience which is relevant to our subject. The result is this concluding chapter.

What you have read so far was based upon my experience attending the est Standard Training, the ten sessions of the Postgraduate Series, along with reading a number of books about est, coupled with a life-time of Christian experience and ten years of work with teachings on the third level. Through all of this I had experienced an expanding transformation of my ability to experience living on higher levels of completeness and satisfaction. Yet there was no doubt in my mind that transformation of the self from content to context had not been experienced. I had enjoyed some peak experiences along the way and I had demonstrated some elements involved in the shift in consciousness, yet not what Werner was describing as the transformation of self. Today, the story is different. The difference came about through a much less known est experience called the Communication Workshop.

Every mind is uniquely programmed. There is no ONE way to crack the complex combination each of us has created for the illusion of psychological survival. As we have mentioned, Jesus taught his special disciples for three years without getting them "off it." It took "total disaster" to do that. Down through the ages, teachers of this wisdom have contrived such

166

mind-blowing experiences, called initiations. If the process worked, the student was then an initiate—a beginner. Actual transformation might then follow.

We have seen that the Standard Training is designed to function as an initiation. It worked that way for me. Then the ten weekly sessions of the Postgraduate Series was a continuation of that process. I was looking forward to attending some of the other series, such as "Be Here Now," "What's So," "About Sex," "About Money," "est and Life," "Self-expression" or "The Body." I found the Postgraduate Series right on, yet as I listened to the sharing and the skillful work of the instructor in bringing the people back to source, I wondered how much of this powerfully straight "stuff" was getting through the quagmire of our minds. At the last session, I got my answer. We were divided up into sharing groups of seven and asked to take 2-1/2 minutes to describe our own experience during the ten weeks.

The one in our group who volunteered to be first was a handsome man in his thirties, delighted with the chance to lead off. He told us that he had at first found the series dull and anticlimactic in comparison to the training. He was so bored he skipped some of the sessions. Then, three weeks from the end, he personally experienced the reality of everyone being perfect—for where they are, who they are and doing what they are doing. He gave details of how he experienced their perfection, describing the delight he had enjoyed during the three following weeks, experiencing all these perfect people.

A young man to his right was next. His articulate report was very different yet no less marvelous. By the time each of us had spoken and the general

sharing of the entire room was concluded, there was
no doubt in my mind that the process started in the
training was continued and accelerated in the
graduate seminar. Some were very frank about their
not finding anything different, yet, as myself, so many
were experiencing greatly increased aliveness.

Then after returning to my home in New Mexico
and writing the preceding part of the book—which
was quite an expanding experience in itself—my wife
and I signed up for The Communication Workshop.
About all I knew about it was the brief comments we
have quoted by Werner in his "Transformation of
est" talk. You might recall that he said, "When you
find out what communication really is, the first thing
you discover is that you don't have any."

We went to California a few days early so that we
could also attend a one-evening Educators Workshop.
It was a great opportunity to listen to those on the
various levels of education share their discoveries
about what happens when teachers really become
responsible as source. Several of those who shared
mentioned the Communication Workshop and what it
had meant to them. One person remarked that he had
resisted almost to the end the facing of those barriers
which were between him and commmunication. After
we heard such comments, we began to appreciate that
this workshop was something very powerful. Even
then, we were surprised at what we found.

I already realized Werner had found that agape-
love and communications are really part and parcel
of the same experience, so I expected his workshop on
communication would be about agape. I knew that I
had a fairly useful conceptualization of agape-love,
just as I had a good understanding that everyone is

really perfect for here and now, yet I also realized that these aspects of seeing were not really experienced experiences. As Werner would say, they were more often non-experienced experiences. In other words, I was experiencing the conceptualization of the experience. That is what the mind is good at.

The Communication Workshop, taught by two regular trainers, was as intensive as the training. The schedule was for forty hours, covering Thursday and Friday evenings and all day Saturday and Sunday, ending each evening at about midnight. The first part of the workshop made it very clear that what we ordinarily call communications is really manipulation—our favorite pastime. Then the rest of the workshop was to enable us to complete the experience of our barriers to true communication as they arose in the processes and as they would arise in the process of life itself. What surprised me most was that much of the data dealt extensively with the meaning of "self" as context. It was a massive assault on the barriers to understanding what and who we are. It was heavy. We were reminded frequently to just stay with the data and not try to believe or disbelieve it, let alone really understand it, because it cannot be understood. We were to just get in touch with our experience of the notions as a point of view. This material, which is only barely introduced in the training, was demonstrated, illustrated, amplified, organized and then worked into a number of processes.

There would be little value in going into the content of the data here. Although the general picture was not new to me, the working elements of it were totally new. Also, we were reminded that the ideas, as concepts, are no more valuable than what we already "know." In fact, I was realizing even while being fascinated with the material that this data or any data, by itself, was not going to do it. There was no question in my mind that Werner had designed this workshop to deal directly with our barriers to more than communications. The Standard Training is about transformation of our ability to experience experience. This workshop is about the transformation of the self to directly experience the Self.

When we completed the workshop, I felt satisfaction and completeness, yet was still bewildered by what Werner had prepared. It was strange. The trainers had said that the workshop is like it is because it starts a process that works. Yet, to be truthful, it really did not seem to be like it would "work"—at least not at the time, not on the level of transformation of the self. That came two days later.

As Werner says, transformation is. It has no end. When an experience of enlightenment comes to an end, it is at best a peak experience. So, for sure, on the following Tuesday I had at least a peak experience and possibly much more. There has been nothing like it in my whole life. Along with it came a "high" which lasted only hours yet the "point of view" experienced at that time continues to be "bankable." In other words, I find that I can draw upon the insight of that experience at will.

We were driving home to New Mexico through the Arizona desert. All of a sudden, it ALL came together. What I had been contemplating and conceptualizing over these many years of searching WAS. I had ceased some time ago to anticipate it. Transformation was just a state that had a name and I had not yet moved through the barriers to experiencing it.

Now, there were no barriers. Relationship, history, individuals, institutions, principles, being, life—all kinds of elements to existence began to move together into a total perfection, completeness, union and meaning.

I began to experience that the world of effect—nothing/everything—was coexisting with Source—everything/nothing. I saw that intention is all there is. As I looked out over the desert, up at the clouds, down the highway, around the car, I saw intention manifest in the world of effect. Every manifestation in the universe of stimulus/response is nothing but IN-TENTION, the intention of creation, experiencing, being—you, me, them, us, everything. Creating is intending. God is not intending, God is INTEN-TION. True intention cannot exist in the world of stimulus/response, for true intention is source, not effect. Effect is plural. Source is singular. Self is Source.

I saw that I, as Source, had taken my position and identity, creating me exactly the way I am, to do exactly what I am doing, win or lose. As my attention included the Christian churches, I saw how they were exactly what they were intended to be at this time and place, win or lose. At the same moment I saw the church which I had been so loyal to for so many years and had finally left. All the questions I had about it were completely resolved. I saw how perfect it was, how complete for the job it was intended to do and not to do. It all came from experiencing who I am, who everybody is, what everything is. And "I" was the total source of that intention, just as you and you and you are. No longer would I find it necessary to work from the outside.

It is true that this experience did not feel like anything, did not look like anything and was not a sensation at all. There were sensations which paralleled it, yet were separate from it. It was space, total context. It was not anything which made me better or superior to anyone. It was just space which went beyond division, duality, opposites and all the other things which do with right-wrong, good-evil and the rest of such knowledge. It was so clear, clean, bright and whole. It was a miracle.

est defines a miracle as an intention which is put out into the universe and is then materialized in the world of effect. The process of both Christianity and est is to enable one to function at the level of intention rather than at the level of stimulus/response. When people graduate from The est Standard Training, they are given a little booklet of sayings. One item is the following:

> One creates from nothing.
>
> If you try to create from something you're just changing something.
>
> So in order to create something you first have to be able to create nothing.
>
> To make sure a person doesn't find out who he is, convince him that he can't really make anything disappear.
>
> All that's left then is to resist, solve, fix, help or change things.
>
> That's trying to make something out of something.

Jesus taught total creative power through faith. Time after time he made such statements as "If ye have faith and doubt not, ye shall say unto this mountain, Be thou removed, and be thou cast into the sea; it shall be done. And ALL THINGS, WHAT-SOEVER YE SHALL ASK in prayer, believing, ye shall receive." There are no limitations, no reservations, no conditions—except one! Doubt! And that, of course, is the catch, for the carnal man (sincere as the devil, of course) tries to have "no doubt" in his double mind. The simple fact is that as soon as the double mind makes anything important, it must have doubt. We call it being anxious. As we discussed in the chapter on the illusion of faith, a person with a double mind may discover ways to get the mind "tranced out" enough to close down the doubting side and then ZAP! It happens. The miracle is then taken as proof that he does not have a double mind.

Real faith is simply INTENTION, making up the mind. The double mind debates. The single mind chooses. Actually, the single mind is the self. The double mind struggles for agreement which it calls communication. The single mind creates intention and acknowledges it as communion. When a person does not know who he is, he does not have true communication even with himself. People live outside and away from themselves even while they think they are their bodies. They are the effect of their ideas of the past, the future, their ideals, beliefs, feelings, sensations and appearances.

Christ acknowledged that he was the creator of ALL creation. That meant that he knew that he had created his own body, just exactly the way it was. He had created a body that could feel pain, sweat, hunger, weariness, wounds, cold, etc. Isaiah had seen that Christ would not be particularly handsome, so he must have looked rather ordinary. Yet what he was was exactly what he had intended his body and mind to be. He was not perfect because he fit everyone's ideals. He was perfect because he was exactly what he had intended.

Communion, which is the real meaning of communication, is the total acceptance of everything from the point of view of being its source—the nature of Christ—that it is exactly the way it is intended to be or it would not be what it is. Therefore it is perfectly according to plan—My plan, YOUR plan. The experience of communication is to consciously recreate what IS THE WAY IT IS. This is communion—agape-love. This is life beyond effect, life as context rather than content, life beyond distance, time and place. Eternal and Everlasting Life is without distance, time and place, beyond the world of effect in the realm of BEING. It is the alpha and the omega, the beginning and the end, all the same. It is not something that one can understand. There is no way for the mind of effect to understand it. However, life as self can and does experience it. To do so is an entirely new existence, called the spiritual man.

TRANSITION

It has been my intention to show how the real, hidden teachings of Christianity can expand and deepen the value a person can receive from est, and also, that est can expand and deepen the value a person can receive from Christianity. Both directions have been so for me.

In closing, I want to discuss the fact that in est, one will experience many things which are not "nice." They are all there by design. The purpose is not to reduce anyone's niceness; but to move one to a higher, more genuine level of real decency and integrity. One does this only by passing through the barriers which make up self-righteousness, bigotry, resistance and intolerance—all of which come from fear, not love. The training allows us the opportunity to get in touch with where our "niceness" comes from.

The est training is designed to function as a "third degree," calling us on our shallowness. This is why many will at first experience the training as being profane, negative, dictatorial, unsympathetic, domineering and arrogant. As I was taking the training, realizing the "method-in-the-madness" and also appreciating the shock some were experiencing, I thought about the time Jesus gave his sharp and damning denunciation of the "greatest and most revered" men in Israel. Even worse, he did it in the holy temple to a great multitude of worshippers and repeated the challenge a dozen times. "Woe unto you, scribes, Pharisees, hypocrites! Ye blind guides . . . Ye fools . . . Ye serpents, ye generation of vipers."[1] Within a week, they had him dead, or so they thought.

Jesus warned us too, when he said, "Woe unto you when all men speak well of you."[2] The reason may be two-fold: (1) when we are aligned with the world we are not aligned with him; (2) life without confrontation really does not go anywhere. So to the est graduate, may I invite you to consider the opportunity to participate in the transformation of institution—in the process called Church. To the active Christian, I will say that the more you have really experienced the experience of Christ, the more you will discover Self in the experience of est. If you go there to judge it, what you will get is $300 worth of judging. If you go there to test and resist it, you will get $300 worth of testing and resistance. However, if you go there with no baggage but the self, follow instructions and take what you get, there is not enough money in the whole world to pay for what you get.

1. Matt. 23:13-39
2. Luke 6:26